The Edict

A Study of the Book of Esther

Written by Robin Ivins

How to Use this Study

Pray. Ask the Lord to reveal truth from His Word.

Read. Start with the scripture. You will find it at the beginning of each chapter.

Observe. What is God teaching you? What did you notice in the passage? Did anything stand out to you? Highlight, underline, and circle those things.

Read. Finally, read the chapter that coincides with the scripture passage. I encourage you to search on your own before reading my thoughts.

Apply. Consider if there is something in the passage that can be applied to your life or circumstance.

Journal. Write those things down. Either within the pages of this book or in another notebook, write what you are learning. Write what God reveals to your heart.

Pray. Thank the Lord for all that He has revealed to you. Praise Him for the blessings. Thank Him for His goodness. Tell Him your needs. Tell Him your hopes and dreams. Thank Him for hearing your prayer.

My child, listen to what I say, and treasure my commands.
Tune your ears to wisdom, and concentrate on understanding.
Cry out for insight, and ask for understanding.
Search for them as you would for silver;
seek them like hidden treasures.

Then you will understand what it means to fear the LORD
and you will gain knowledge of God.

For the LORD grants wisdom!
From his mouth come knowledge and understanding.
He grants a treasure of common sense to the honest.
He is a shield to those who walk with integrity.
He guards the paths of the just
And protects those who are faithful to him.

Then you will understand what is right, just, and fair,
And you will find the right way to go.

For wisdom will enter your heart,
And knowledge will fill you with joy.
Wise choices will watch over you.
Understanding will keep you safe.

Proverbs 2:1-11

Table of Contents

Acknowledgments

The Book of Esther has always interested and intrigued me. Many years ago, when I first realized my love of writing and wanted to develop the skill to be shared with others, I chose *For Such a Time as This* as the title of what I hoped would be a ministry. Little did I know that my poems and journaling would evolve into a desire to dive headfirst into a book of the Bible *for such a time as this!*

In writing *The Edict, A Study of the Book of Esther,* my practice has been to prayerfully meditate on the word for myself, then journal my own insights before considering the teaching of others. Digging deeper, my thoughts were influenced and enhanced by the research and wisdom of Drew Crowell's teaching. Specifically, and with his permission, I have used notes from Drew Crowell's teaching in writing this study.

From Drew Crowell, I have learned the importance of putting myself into the story. God gave us an imagination. We can use it to get into the setting, the time period, and the nitty-gritty of what life was like at the time. We can ask God for wisdom. Seek to understand the perspective of those in the story. Seek to understand God's perspective. With our imagination, we can look around. What is being described? Where did this happen? What was the culture of the time? What are the sights and sounds? Can you imagine the atmosphere? How does the air feel? Is there a fragrance in the air? What do your senses reveal? We can also ask: How does what I am learning apply to my own circumstance? What does this mean for my life?

Spending time approaching God's Word like this has greatly enhanced my writing! It has opened my mind to new thoughts and led me to realize, in a deeper way, that there is a purpose in everything. Every word of God is connected to another. Every life is a small part of the larger story. Every detail has a purpose. There is so much more for us to know and understand. God's Word is hidden treasure, and as His children, we need to search it out. I challenge you to find some treasure for yourself!

> *".. they received the word with all eagerness, examining the Scriptures daily to see if these things were so."* Acts 17:11 ESV

Drew Crowell, thank you for challenging minds and hearts to get into God's Word and examine it in a deeper way.

Salvatore and Annmarie D'Amico, thank you for introducing me to Drew.

Steve Young, thank you for your words of encouragement along the way.

My husband, **Bob Ivins,** thank you for your support in every way every day. I am grateful.

Prelude

The following six pages provide historical back-ground information to lend a deeper under-standing to this study.

Reading through pages 12-17 is not necessary to the study, but I believe it will be helpful in understanding the times, people, and culture.

I pray you will be blessed!

The Backstory...

There had been four hundred years of Israel being ruled by judges since the exodus out of Egypt. Following the ways of the cultures around them, Israel decided they needed a king. They approached the prophet Samuel with this idea.

> *Finally, all the elders of Israel met at Ramah to discuss the matter with Samuel. "Look," they told him, "you are now old, and your sons are not like you. Give us a king to judge us like all the other nations have." Samuel was displeased with their request and went to the LORD for guidance.*
> 1 Samuel 8:4-6

God was their king, but they were not satisfied with God's plan.

> *Do everything they say to you," the LORD replied, "for they are rejecting me, not you. They don't want me to be their king any longer. Ever since I brought them from Egypt they have continually abandoned me and followed other gods. And now they are giving you the same treatment.*
> 1 Samuel 8:7-8

So God gave them what they asked for. Even though it wasn't what was best for them and even though He knew it would be their downfall. God does that sometimes. He does not force His will on us. He gives us a free will. He desires that we submit to His plan and carry out His will, but He will not force us to do so. When God backs away to let us have our own way, that is a frightening place to be.

Israel's first three kings were Saul, David, and Solomon. King Solomon imposed a heavy tax on the northern tribes. After his death, when his son continued the taxation his father had implemented, the northern tribes revolted. In the end, ten tribes became Israel, ruled by the tribe of Ephraim, and the remaining three became Judah, ruled by the tribe of Judah, of the house of David. That is how God's chosen people were divided into two kingdoms. Israel was to the north, and Judah was to the south.

In the following 220 years, the northern kingdom of **Israel** had 20 wicked kings. ***There was not one godly king among them***. The people followed in their wickedness, and because of it, God allowed them to be taken into captivity by Assyria. This part of Israel's history can be found in 2 Kings 17.

Then the king of Assyria invaded the entire land, and for three years he besieged the city of Samaria. Finally, in the ninth year of King Hoshea's reign, Samaria fell, and the people of Israel were exiled to Assyria. They were settled in colonies in Halah, along the banks of the Habor River in Gozan, and in the cities of the Medes.

This disaster came upon the people of Israel because they worshiped other gods. They sinned against the LORD their God, who had brought them safely out of Egypt and had rescued them from the power of Pharaoh, the king of Egypt. They had followed the practices of the pagan nations the LORD had driven from the land ahead of them, as well as the practices the kings of Israel had introduced. The people of Israel had also secretly done many things that were not pleasing to the LORD their God. They built pagan shrines for themselves in all their towns, from the smallest outpost to the largest walled city. They set up sacred pillars and Asherah poles at the top of every hill and under every green tree. They offered sacrifices on all the hilltops, just like the nations the LORD had driven from the land ahead of them. So the people of Israel had done many evil things, arousing the LORD's anger. Yes, they worshiped idols, despite the LORD's specific and repeated warnings.

Again and again the LORD had sent his prophets and seers to warn both Israel and Judah: "Turn from all your evil ways. Obey my commands and decrees—the entire law that I commanded your ancestors to obey, and that I gave you through my servants the prophets." But the Israelites would not listen. They were as stubborn as their ancestors who had refused to believe in the LORD their God. They rejected his decrees and the covenant he had made with their ancestors, and they despised all his warnings. They worshiped worthless idols, so they became worthless themselves. They followed the example of the nations around them, disobeying the LORD's command not to imitate them.

They rejected all the commands of the LORD their God and made two calves from metal. They set up an Asherah pole and worshiped Baal and all the forces of heaven. They even sacrificed their own sons and daughters in the fire. They consulted fortune-tellers and practiced sorcery and sold themselves to evil, arousing the LORD's anger.

_Because the L_ORD **_was very angry with Israel, he swept them away from his presence. Only the tribe of Judah remained in the land._**

2 Kings 17:5–18

Let's now look at Judah. Judah also had 20 kings. Roughly one-half were good. Only four of them are remembered as "godly." These four were outstanding in their commitment and obedience to all that God commanded. Their names were Asa, Jehoshaphat, Hezekiah, and Josiah. Each of these kings removed the "high places," putting an end to the worship of idols.

King Hezekiah was strong in leading the people of Judah in obedience to God.

> *...He did what was pleasing in the L*ORD*'s sight...Hezekiah trusted in the L*ORD*, the God of Israel. There was no one like him among all the kings of Judah, either before or after his time. He remained faithful to the Lord in everything, and he carefully obeyed all the commands the Lord had given to Moses. So the Lord was with him, and Hezekiah was successful in everything he did.* 2 Kings 18:3, 5-7

But over time, Hezekiah became complacent and presumptuous. Instead of trusting God to intervene when Assyria sieged Judah, Hezekiah sought to appease the king of Assyria with gifts. He took from the temple treasury, the temple itself, and the palace all the silver and gold and gave them to the King of Assyria. Hezekiah presumed that his solution was good enough. He didn't call on the Lord, God. This resulted in the Assyrian king making a mockery of him to the people of Judah by basically saying, "People, why would you listen to Hezekiah and trust your God when even he doesn't seem to trust God? Come follow Assyrian ways, and all will be well."

> *Manasseh was twelve years old when he became king, and he reigned in Jerusalem fifty-five years. He did what was evil in the L*ORD*'s sight, following the detestable practices of the pagan nations that the L*ORD *had driven from the land ahead of the Israelites. He rebuilt the pagan shrines his father, Hezekiah, had broken down. He constructed altars for the images of Baal and set up Asherah poles. He also bowed before all the powers of the heavens and worshiped them.*
>
> *He built pagan altars in the Temple of the L*ORD*, the place where*

the LORD had said, "My name will remain in Jerusalem forever." He built these altars for all the powers of the heavens in both courtyards of the LORD's Temple. Manasseh also sacrificed his own sons in the fire in the valley of Ben-Hinnom. He practiced sorcery, divination, and witchcraft, and he consulted with mediums and psychics. He did much that was evil in the LORD's sight, arousing his anger.

Manasseh even took a carved idol he had made and set it up in God's Temple, the very place where God had told David and his son Solomon: "My name will be honored forever in this Temple and in Jerusalem—the city I have chosen from among all the tribes of Israel. If the Israelites will be careful to obey my commands—all the laws, decrees, and regulations given through Moses—I will not send them into exile from this land that I set aside for your ancestors." But Manasseh led the people of Judah and Jerusalem to do even more evil than the pagan nations that the Lord had destroyed when the people of Israel entered the land.   2 Chronicles 33:1-9

The Lord allowed Manasseh to be captured and carried off to Babylon. There, he was tortured. It was also there—in great affliction—that Manasseh humbled himself, prayed, and finally knew that the Lord is God. God, in His great mercy, saved Manasseh. When King Manasseh passed away, his son Amon became king in his place. Amon led the people in rebellion and wickedness. After only two years, some of his own servants assassinated him. That was when his young son, the godly King Josiah, took his place.

Josiah was eight years old when he became king, and he reigned in Jerusalem thirty-one years. He did what was pleasing in the LORD's sight and followed the example of his ancestor David. He did not turn away from doing what was right.

During the eighth year of his reign, while he was still young, Josiah began to seek the God of his ancestor David. Then in the twelfth year he began to purify Judah and Jerusalem, destroying all the pagan shrines, the Asherah poles, and the carved idols and cast images.
                    2 Chronicles 34:1-3

Never before had there been a king like Josiah, who turned to the Lord with all his heart and soul and strength, obeying all the laws of Moses. And there has never been a king like him since.

2 Kings 23:25

God gave Judah one last revival. It came through the wisdom of the young man-king, Josiah. Judgment, however, was on its way. God had had enough.

> *Even so, the LORD was very angry with Judah because of all the wicked things Manasseh had done to provoke him. For the Lord said, "I will also banish Judah from my presence just as I have banished Israel. And I will reject my chosen city of Jerusalem and the temple where my name was to be honored."* 2 Kings 23:26-27

Two more wicked kings ruled in Judah, and then 2 Kings 24:1-4 tells us that when Nebuchadnezzar, King of Babylon, came up against Judah, the final king, Jehoiakim, surrendered and paid tribute to him for three years. God had warned Judah again and again through many prophets and finally through the prophet Jeremiah, but instead of repenting and turning back to worship of the one true God, the people lashed out at the prophet, seeking to kill him. In response, God sent several nations to attack and destroy Judah. This was the resulting judgment of all that had occurred during the time of Manasseh and the subsequent continued wickedness of Judah as a whole.

✗ ✗ ✗

Israel in Captivity

The 1st Captivity: Daniel 1:3-4. The stories of Daniel, Shadrach, Meshach, and Abednego.

> *Then the king ordered Ashpenaz, his chief of staff, to bring to the palace some of the young men of Judah's royal family and other noble families, who had been brought to Babylon as captives. "Select only strong, healthy, and good-looking young men," he said. "Make sure they are well versed in every branch of learning, are gifted with knowledge and good judgment, and are suited to serve in the royal palace. Train these young men in the language and literature of Babylon.*

The 2nd Captivity: 2 Kings 24:14. The family of Kish (ancestor of Mordecai and Esther).

King Nebuchadnezzar took all of Jerusalem captive, including all the commanders and the best of the soldiers, craftsmen, and artisans— 10,000 in all. Only the poorest people were left in the land.

Esther 2:5-7. Mordecai was great grandson of Kish. Hadassah, later named Esther, was Mordecai's cousin.

At that time there was a Jewish man in the fortress of Susa whose name was Mordecai son of Jair. He was from the tribe of Benjamin and was a descendant of Kish and Shimei. His family had been among those who, with King Jehoiachin of Judah, had been exiled from Jerusalem to Babylon by King Nebuchadnezzar. This man had a very beautiful and lovely young cousin, Hadassah, who was also called Esther. When her father and mother died, Mordecai adopted her into his family and raised her as his own daughter.

The 3rd Captivity: 2 Chronicles 36:11-20. God allows the kingdom of Judah to fall to Babylon.

Zedekiah was twenty-one years old when he became king, and he reigned in Jerusalem eleven years. But Zedekiah did what was evil in the sight of the Lord his God, and he refused to humble himself when the prophet Jeremiah spoke to him directly from the Lord. He also rebelled against King Nebuchadnezzar, even though he had taken an oath of loyalty in God's name. Zedekiah was a hard and stubborn man, refusing to turn to the Lord, the God of Israel.

Likewise, all the leaders of the priests and the people became more and more unfaithful. They followed all the pagan practices of the surrounding nations, desecrating the Temple of the Lord that had been consecrated in Jerusalem.

The Lord, the God of their ancestors, repeatedly sent his prophets to warn them, for he had compassion on his people and his Temple. But the people mocked these messengers of God and despised their words. They scoffed at the prophets until the Lord's anger could no longer be restrained and nothing could be done.

God used Nebuchadnezzar to discipline His children. He cannot let sin go without consequences. God is always working to lead us back to obedience and a right relationship with Him.

So the LORD brought the king of Babylon against them. The Babylonians killed Judah's young men, even chasing after them into the Temple. They had no pity on the people, killing both young men and young women, the old and the infirm. God handed all of them over to Nebuchadnezzar. The king took home to Babylon all the articles, large and small, used in the Temple of God, and the treasures from both the LORD's Temple and from the palace of the king and his officials. Then his army burned the Temple of God, tore down the walls of Jerusalem, burned all the palaces, and completely destroyed everything of value. The few who survived were taken as exiles to Babylon, and they became servants to the king and his sons until the kingdom of Persia came to power.

This brings us to our story. The setting is the kingdom of Persia. The dates are 486 to 465 BC, and it is here that we will venture into our study of the Book of Esther.

Part 1

The Edict

"Could This Be God's Way?"

"...Vashti shall come no more before
King Ahasuerus; and let the king give
her royal position to
another who is better than she..."

Esther 1:19 NKJV

Long Celebration!

Read: Esther 1:1-9

These events happened in the days of King Xerxes, who reigned over 127 provinces stretching from India to Ethiopia. At that time Xerxes ruled his empire from his royal throne at the fortress of Susa. In the third year of his reign, he gave a banquet for all his nobles and officials. He invited all the military officers of Persia and Media as well as the princes and nobles of the provinces. The celebration lasted 180 days—a tremendous display of the opulent wealth of his empire and the pomp and splendor of his majesty.

When it was all over, the king gave a banquet for all the people, from the greatest to the least, who were in the fortress of Susa. It lasted for seven days and was held in the courtyard of the palace garden. The courtyard was beautifully decorated with white cotton curtains and blue hangings, which were fastened with white linen cords and purple ribbons to silver rings embedded in marble pillars. Gold and silver couches stood on a mosaic pavement of porphyry, marble, mother-of-pearl, and other costly stones.

Drinks were served in gold goblets of many designs, and there was an abundance of royal wine, reflecting the king's generosity. By edict of the king, no limits were placed on the drinking, for the king had instructed all his palace officials to serve each man as much as he wanted.

At the same time, Queen Vashti gave a banquet for the women in the royal palace of King Xerxes.

In the days of King Xerxes. Who was Xerxes? King Xerxes (Greek), also known in scripture as King Ahasuerus (Hebrew), ruled in Persia from 486 to 465 BC. His empire was vast. It included 127 provinces stretching from present-day India to Ethiopia. This included the regions of the Medes, Persians, Babylonians, and Arabs. Xerxes ruled from his throne at the fortress of Susa, 220 miles east of Babylon.

Most of the known world was conquered during the reign of King Nebuchadnezzar. In time, Belshazzar inherited the empire. His story is in the book of Daniel, chapter 5.

At that time Xerxes ruled his empire from his royal throne at the fortress of Susa.

Continuing on in Daniel chapters 5 and 6, and Ezra chapter 1, we learn about the succession of kings leading up to Xerxes reign. They were Darius the Mede, Cyrus the Great, Darius 1, and finally Xerxes. King Xerxes inherited great wealth and a vast empire.

Xerxes ruled from his royal throne. This was a king of great pride and arrogance. Full of self-importance, he desired to be honored, praised, and even envied. To fill this need for approval and admiration, he planned a six-month-long celebration and invited everyone of any significance to join him. Invited were not only his own nobles and officials but also military officers, princes, and nobles from other provinces.

This party was not just to impress. We know from history that part of Xerxes' plan was to sway the opinion of these high-ranking officials so they would agree to invade Greece. The invasion of Greece led by his father in earlier years had failed, and Xerxes planned to take Greece, then all of current day Europe. He planned to be king of the world! So, this was ***a tremendous display of the opulent wealth of his empire and the pomp and splendor of his majesty.*** Xerxes had it all and wasn't afraid to show it. For 180 days. A six-month-long party!

And that wasn't enough! To make sure that no one missed an opportunity to admire his greatness, at the end of the 180 days, he ordered a second banquet lasting 7 days for all the ordinary people who lived in the fortress of Susa. The palace must have been overflowing with guests, as we read that this party was held in the courtyard of the palace garden. Everything was done in excess. We read of linen curtains, marble columns, silver and gold couches, mosaic pavement of costly stones, and golden goblets of royal wine without limit. The guests, many of them princes with wealth, would realize they could not compare to the majestic opulence of King Xerxes!

It seems it was all about the king. *His* empire. *His* throne. *His* reign. *His* plans. *His* wealth. *His* majesty. *His* praise. *His* banquet. *His* generosity. *His* palace. *His* queen.

Her banquet. This is where we meet Vashti.

Today's passage ends with the banquet hosted by Queen Vashti. This was a banquet for women. It coincided with the king's celebration. These were likely the wives of the royalty and officials who were being entertained by Xerxes.

We are not told much about Vashti's banquet, but if it lasted as long as the men's, it must have been every bit as impressive. Maybe Vashti was a little self-focused herself. We will learn more about her as we continue the story.

Faith comes by hearing and hearing by the Word of God.

At this point, we could choose to merely accept these people as characters in a story. We could be impressed with their majesty and splendor, without really understanding the significance of their lives. Why did they do the things they did? How can this possibly make any difference to us? It is by trying to understand in a deeper way, that we are able to uncover important life lessons.

I may not have great wealth, a vast empire, or even servants, but I know that I have certainly sat on the throne of my life, reigning, and promoting self-praise. Something I have learned about myself is that I can be just as self-absorbed and arrogant as King Xerxes. Don't we all go there at times?

This is why I need my nose in God's Word. It helps me to remember that the only One worthy to sit on the throne of my heart is the Lord Jesus.

Everything good in my life is from Him, through Him, because of Him, and for Him. All the good in my life is to be used for His glory. Only Jesus is worthy of all the praise. It is *His* generosity, *His* wealth, *His* creation, *His* laws, and *His* praise. My heart is *His* rightful throne. Life is spiritually rich and beautiful when I let King Jesus reign.

What do you think? What did God reveal to you as you read this passage? Is there anything here that should impact who you are and how you follow Christ today? Spend some time re-reading and finding your own treasure.

This is where you will begin your journal of the Book of Esther.

My Treasure From God's Word...

_____

_____

_____

_____

_____

_____

_____

_____

_____

_____

_____

_____

_____

_____

_____

_____

_____

_____

_____

_____

_____

"My child, pay attention to what I say. Listen carefully to my words. Don't lose sight of them. Let them penetrate deep into your heart." Proverbs 4:20-21

Trophy Wife

Read: Esther 1:10-12

On the seventh day of the feast, when King Xerxes was in high spirits because of the wine, he told the seven eunuchs who attended him—Mehuman, Biztha, Harbona, Bigtha, Abagtha, Zethar, and Carcas—to bring Queen Vashti to him with the royal crown on her head. He wanted the nobles and all the other men to gaze on her beauty, for she was a very beautiful woman. But when they conveyed the king's order to Queen Vashti, she refused to come. This made the king furious, and he burned with anger.

This part of the passage opens on the seventh day of the king's banquet. All involved were in **high spirits** because of the wine. Near Xerxes were seven eunuchs. A close look at those names may give you a smile. I am sure my pronunciation is off, but for now, reading them in English is quite entertaining. "Mehuman" and "Carcas" are especially amusing to me!

The atmosphere was luxurious and party-like. Dripping with wine, the men were uninhibited. Loud, rowdy laughter, and boasting likely filled the air. King Xerxes had definitely impressed these men, and now he wanted to take it a step further. He decided to show off his queen. He would display her in all her beauty for all to see. He ordered the eunuchs, all seven, to bring Vashti. They were to make sure she had her royal crown so that all would see and know the extent of her majestic splendor—this queen who *belonged* to Xerxes.

I wonder why he ordered not one, but seven eunuchs to go retrieve her. Did it take that many to assist her in making herself presentable? Did she bring a lot of items with her when she came into the presence of the king? Maybe her long, flowing gown was heavy, and men were needed to carry it as it trailed behind her. It does not say. We can only guess. Whatever the reason, he sent seven men. These were seven "safe" men. Men whose manhood had been forfeited for the service of the king, and therefore, could be trusted in all of their dealings with his queen.

Let's take a little sidestep at this point and think about Xerxes' motives in sending for Vashti. We know he wanted to show her off, but did he also love her? Did he enjoy her company? He was seeking to promote himself through

Queen Vashti...refused to come. This made the king furious, and he burned with anger.

her. He was hungry for social power and the respect of men. Women seek love. Men seek respect. God's model for men is to protect, provide, and pursue. When this occurs, a woman feels loved. She responds to love. I am not sure that Vashti experienced love from Xerxes. Yes, he protected her—for his own interests. Yes, he provided for her—for his own interests. There likely was not a lot of pursuing going on as everything and everyone *belonged* to the king.

Had he not been in such high spirits, perhaps he would have stopped to realize that this request may not be agreeable to the queen. Maybe he would have reconsidered. People often make bad decisions when they have been drinking and reveling with friends. Things that usually give them pause may seem acceptable. The consequences of such actions may seem of no consequence at the time.

The Bible records many stories of people who made costly mistakes that were the result of excessive drinking. Lot was tricked into sleeping with his two daughters (Genesis 19), and Jacob honeymooned with Leah in the darkness, all the while thinking she was Rachel, his chosen wife (Genesis 29). Then there was David's sin with Bathsheba. David was attempting to hide his sin by getting Uriah drunk so that he would sleep with his wife (2 Samuel 11). What a sad, downward spiral! Yes, when drinking to excess is involved, things often come to an unhappy end.

So, what of Queen Vashti? Whatever her reasons, she refused to come at the command of the king. This did not go well at all. King Xerxes was not accustomed to being refused anything. People were not permitted to tell him no—especially a woman. This demonstrated disrespect. It was humiliating to Xerxes, and he was enraged.

Love and respect are the Creator's plan and design. His way is perfect. We are wise to seek to understand and live within His plan and design. His way is the way of love, significance, protection, fulfillment, and peace.

God created men and women with differing emotional needs. While a woman's primary need is love, respect is the primary need for men. This is how God designed us. Why is it important to understand this? It is because most of us look at the needs of others from our own perspective, and we can overlook what is most valued.

A woman must change her perspective to understand the greatest needs of the men in her life. Men thrive on *respect*. Women demonstrate their respect for men through words, attitudes, and actions. Likewise, a man must change his perspective to understand the greatest needs of a woman. Women thrive on *love*. Men demonstrate their love for women by protecting, providing for, and pursuing them.

What is God saying to you as you read this section? Did you find any new insights?

My Treasure From God's Word...

_____

_____

_____

_____

_____

_____

_____

_____

_____

_____

_____

_____

_____

_____

_____

_____

_____

_____

_____

_____

_____

"So again I say, each man must love his wife as he loves
himself, and the wife must respect her husband."
Ephesians 5:33

Saving Face

Read: Esther 1:13-22

He immediately consulted with his wise advisers, who knew all the Persian laws and customs, for he always asked their advice. The names of these men were Carshena, Shethar, Admatha, Tarshish, Meres, Marsena, and Memucan—seven nobles of Persia and Media. They met with the king regularly and held the highest positions in the empire.

"What must be done to Queen Vashti?" the king demanded. "What penalty does the law provide for a queen who refuses to obey the king's orders, properly sent through his eunuchs?"

Memucan answered the king and his nobles, "Queen Vashti has wronged not only the king but also every noble and citizen through-out your empire. Women everywhere will begin to despise their husbands when they learn that Queen Vashti has refused to appear before the king. Before this day is out, the wives of all the king's nobles throughout Persia and Media will hear what the queen did and will start treating their husbands the same way. There will be no end to their contempt and anger.

"So if it please the king, we suggest that you issue a written decree, a law of the Persians and Medes that cannot be revoked. It should order that Queen Vashti be forever banished from the presence of King Xerxes, and that the king should choose another queen more worthy than she. When this decree is published throughout the king's vast empire, husbands everywhere, whatever their rank, will receive proper respect from their wives!"

The king and his nobles thought this made good sense, so he fol-lowed Memucan's counsel. He sent letters to all parts of the em-pire, to each province in its own script and language, proclaiming that every man should be the ruler of his own home and should say whatever he pleases.

He sent letters to all parts of the empire, to each province in its own script and language, proclaiming that every man should be the ruler of his own home and should say whatever he pleases.

Today we are delving deeper into the character of King Xerxes. If he had known his wife as he should, he likely could have avoided this problem. Why was he so angry? It was because Vashti's refusal to be the object of his *show-and-tell* was causing him to lose face. He felt humiliated. For him, this was an unfamiliar emotion. Insecurity kicked in. The entire party now knew of Vashti's disobedience and disrespect toward the king. Something had to be done.

He called for his wisest advisors. They knew and understood the law. If Xerxes had any *friends*, these would have been them. The king should know the law, especially with regard to his personal life, but Xerxes did not. It seems he did not know much about the laws of his vast empire. He was dependent on others. These self-centered others.

Their perspective is interesting. These advisors were not unbiased in their counsel. They decided that, by disobeying the king, Vashti had wronged every noble and citizen in the entire empire! They viewed this as a personal affront. Now, all women would rise up and disrespect their husbands. This would guarantee humiliation for all men. It appears there was no law for such unprecedented, willful disobedience. Something radical had to be done.

The solution was an edict. An irrevocable and irreversible law to be made by the king.

We know from the story of Daniel, chapter 6, that even if a king wanted to change his mind, the law could not be changed. *"According to the law of the Medes and the Persians, no law that the king signs can be changed."* So there was precedent for lawmaking and law keeping. Whatever law King Xerxes made could not be reversed or changed. So, did he follow the advice and banish his wife forever? Was saving his ego and pride more important than loving and forgiving his wife?

He followed their counsel. They had reasoned that banishing Vashti would prevent rebellion among the women of the kingdom. Women would honor their husbands if Xerxes made Vashti an example of what happens if they do not. His princes, nobles, military officials—all men would respect him for taking a stand against this rebellious and unworthy wife. Apparently, this counsel was pleasing to the king. Proud King Xerxes was saving face.

The edict was written in the language of every province. It was signed, sealed, and delivered throughout the empire. Queen Vashti was to be banished forever. She was never again to enter the presence of her husband, the king. Xerxes would be choosing another wife. *Beautiful Queen Vashti, unloved, was nearly erased.*

How would the story be different if Xerxes had chosen to respond in love to his wife? What if he had been considerate of her needs more than he was concerned about impressing his friends? What if he had gone to her asking why she would not come? Maybe she longed for him to come after her. To pursue her. Maybe she wanted him to do anything to demonstrate that he cared. However, her response may have been a flat-out rebellion. Maybe she just wanted to humiliate him. We don't really know. What if Vashti had chosen, out of respect, to just do what he asked? The outcome would have been quite different. This is not the end of the story. God is always working through the choices of man to bring about His wonderful plan. What is He teaching you today as you consider His Word?

My Treasure From God's Word...

_____

_____

_____

_____

_____

_____

_____

_____

_____

_____

_____

_____

_____

_____

_____

_____

_____

_____

_____

"For the word of God is alive and powerful. It is sharper than the sharpest two-edged sword, cutting between soul and spirit, between joint and marrow. It exposes our inner-most thoughts and desires." Hebrews 4:12

Regrets

Read: Esther 2:1-4

But after Xerxes' anger had subsided, he began thinking about Vashti and what she had done and the decree he had made. So his personal attendants suggested, "Let us search the empire to find beautiful young virgins for the king. Let the king appoint agents in each province to bring these beautiful young women into the royal harem at the fortress of Susa. Hegai, the king's eunuch in charge of the harem, will see that they are all given beauty treatments. After that, the young woman who most pleases the king will be made queen instead of Vashti." This advice was very appealing to the king, so he put the plan into effect.

From the writing of historians we know that nearly four years had passed since Vashti was deposed. Xerxes had carried out his campaign to invade Greece and it had failed. This prideful, self-indulgent king came home in humiliation instead of honor. Once home it seems he finally let go of his anger and started to second-guess his decision. **He began thinking about Vashti.** He thought about what she had done. He thought about what he had done. Had he acted too rashly? The law could not be changed. Could there have been another way?

Have you ever said words in anger that you wished you could take back? Ever made bad decisions in an angry response? Have you behaved in ways that you were later ashamed of? That may be where we find King Xerxes today.

When we rewind the tapes of our minds and replay our anger-filled responses to those we love, what emotions rise to the top? Regret? Shame? Shock that we could be so cruel? Xerxes, head clear from overindulgence and calm in spirit, seems to have sat back and thought, *"What have I done?"*

We have an advantage that Xerxes did not have. We have scriptures to show us how to live. The Bible speaks quite a bit about anger and what to do with it. Let's look at what God says about anger. (The following page allows some space to write your own thoughts.)

"Understand this, my dear brothers and sisters: You must all be quick to listen, slow to speak, and slow to get angry. Human anger does not produce the righteousness God desires." James 1:19-29

1) Slow to get angry. Why? Nothing good comes from anger. God is developing righteousness in us. Human anger interrupts the process.

"People with understanding control their anger; a hot temper shows great foolishness." Proverbs 14:29

2) Anger is an emotion that must be controlled. Why? Uncontrolled anger will result in decisions made, actions taken, and words spoken that cannot be erased.

"Sensible people control their temper; they earn respect by overlooking wrongs." Proverbs 19:11

3) Controlling your temper is sensible. Why? Overlooking a wrong will earn respect.

"And 'don't sin by letting anger control you.'......." Don't let the sun go down while you are still angry, for anger gives a foothold to the devil." Ephesians 4:26

4) Do not let anger control you. Why? It gives Satan free reign in your mind and heart. Words will be said and actions taken that are later regretted.

"Don't use foul or abusive language. Let everything you say be good and helpful, so that your words will be an encouragement to those who hear them."

"Get rid of all bitterness, rage, anger, harsh words, and slander, as well as all types of evil behavior. Instead, be kind to each other, tenderhearted, forgiving one another, just as God through Christ has forgiven you." Ephesians 4:29 and 32

5) Get rid of abusive angry language. Why? You can choose to speak words that give life. Let kindness, a tender heart, and forgiveness rule. Love others like God loves. Be like Jesus.

36

Let's give more thought to King Xerxes. What should he do? His stunningly beautiful queen-wife, companion, and mother of his son (it is believed that Vashti was the mother of his son, Artaxerxes) was gone. Sent away. Banished. His anger and fury had set him on an unexpected course. Seeking to preserve his ego and quell his indignation, he had created a new problem. He no longer had his queen.

His advisors, who demonstrated no care for what this would mean for the king, offered another solution. Since it was to their advantage to keep the king happy, they suggested what should be done. The empire should be searched to find **beautiful, young virgins.**

They were to be brought to the king's harem and given beauty treatments of every sort. Whichever young woman pleased the king the most, would be his new queen. Beautiful, young virgins.

While the edict to banish Vashti had appealed to his pride, this new plan appealed to the king's self-indulgent desires. It pleased the king, and so— the search was on.

✦

Xerxes gave in to anger—and lost his queen. How does anger change you? What impact does unbridled anger have on those around you? Ask the Lord what He is saying to you about anger. Record your thoughts on the next page.

My Treasure From God's Word...

_____

_____

_____

_____

_____

_____

_____

_____

_____

_____

_____

"All Scripture is inspired by God and is useful to teach us what is true and to make us realize what is wrong in our lives. It corrects us when we are wrong and teaches us to do what is right. God uses it to prepare and equip his people to do every good work."
2 Timothy 3:16-17

Taken!

Read: Esther 2:5-9

At that time there was a Jewish man in the fortress of Susa whose name was Mordecai son of Jair. He was from the tribe of Benjamin and was a descendant of Kish and Shimei. His family had been among those who, with King Jehoiachin of Judah, had been exiled from Jerusalem to Babylon by King Nebuchadnezzar. This man had a very beautiful and lovely young cousin, Hadassah, who was also called Esther. When her father and mother died, Mordecai adopted her into his family and raised her as his own daughter.

As a result of the king's decree, Esther, along with many other young women, was brought to the king's harem at the fortress of Susa and placed in Hegai's care. Hegai was very impressed with Esther and treated her kindly. He quickly ordered a special menu for her and provided her with beauty treatments. He also assigned her seven maids specially chosen from the king's palace, and he moved her and her maids into the best place in the harem.

At this point in the story, we are introduced to two new characters. They are Mordecai and his young cousin, Hadassah. We remember that Mordecai was a descendant of the Hebrew king, Saul. He was of the tribe of Benjamin. As mentioned in the backstory, the tribe of Benjamin was one of the three tribes that made up the southern kingdom of Judah. Since his ancestors had lived in captivity since the time of King Nebuchadnezzar, Mordecai was born in Persia. The name Mordecai in Hebrew means *oppressed* or *crushed*. It certainly describes what life in captivity must have been like for the Jews. We will soon learn that the God who allowed His people to be taken into captivity is also the God who is always at work behind the scenes, turning kings hearts to bring His people to repentance of their sin and back into relationship with Him. As it was then, even today, sin has consequences. The consequence of sin is often painful, but God does not waste our pain. He uses it to help us realize our sin and our intense need for Him—if we allow Him.

So Mordecai, a Jewish man, lived in the fortress of Susa. Being the capital city, it was the seat of government and the home of King Xerxes. Mordecai's young cousin was named Hadassah, which in Hebrew means *myrtle tree*.

Esther, along with many other young women, was brought to the king's harem.

The myrtle tree is a symbol of peace, love, and prosperity. Perhaps her parents envisioned a glimmer of hope with the birth of this child! To her peers, she was known by the Persian name Esther, meaning *star,* while in Hebrew it means *bride*. Her names combined define her as *a star or a bride, having characteristics of peace, love, and prosperity.* Quite a predictor of her future, I think! In the sovereignty of God, there are no mistakes.

Through events we are not told, Esther had been orphaned. Even in this sad fact, we see the activity of God. Esther's heavenly Father made sure that she was taken care of. God is a ***"Father to the fatherless"*** and a ***"defender of orphans."*** (Psalm 10:14, 68:5) Esther's parents were gone, but God had her covered. Mordecai adopted her and raised her as his own, but God's sovereign plan for Esther didn't end there!

Acting upon the king's latest decree, agents of the king went throughout every province in search of beautiful young virgins. Of those *taken* we read that Esther, the Jew, was among them. From what we know of decrees during Xerxes' reign, I doubt she was given a choice. Was she enthralled to be among those chosen? Did she feel honored by the possibility of meeting the king? Was she deceived into thinking it was for some other reason? The scripture does not say. It seems to me that, being *taken* by the king's agents and swept away to some place she didn't know—leaving behind all she loved and knew—she would have been upset and frightened.

Taken to the king's harem, Esther's hope of marriage to someone from among her own people was forfeited. She would be destined to spend her life in the king's harem. In a day's time, she had become the property of the king. The writings of the historian Josephus tell us that four hundred young women were taken from the one hundred twenty-seven provinces. The odds of becoming queen were small. Esther could have become angry, bitter, and rebellious, but we do not see that response in her story. We see only humility, grace, and obedience. Although brought to the palace for her outward beauty, this young woman possessed an inward beauty that would soon become evident to all.

She was placed under the direct supervision of Hegai, the overseer of the king's harem. From the start, Esther stood out from the other women. Of all the women, Esther impressed Hegai the most. He treated her kindly, offered her the best foods, gave her unlimited beauty treatments, seven maids, and the best rooms. We have to wonder what the other women thought. This was a highly competitive environment. She was obviously Hegai's choice. Did they resent Esther? Resentment and jealousy would be the expected responses. What might she have experienced? Do you think she believed that God was aware of her circumstances?

How would you feel?

My Treasure From God's Word...

_____

_____

_____

_____

_____

_____

_____

_____

_____

_____

_____

_____

_____

_____

_____

_____

_____

_____

_____

_____

_____

"Do everything without complaining and arguing, so that no one can criticize you. Live clean, innocent lives as children of God, shining like bright lights in a world full of crooked and perverse people." Philippians 2:14–15

Competition

Read: Esther 2:10-15

Esther had not revealed her people or family, for Mordecai had charged her not to reveal it. And every day Mordecai paced in front of the court of the women's quarters, to learn of Esther's welfare and what was happening to her.

Each young woman's turn came to go in to King Ahasuerus after she had completed twelve months' preparation, according to the regulations for the women, for thus were the days of their preparation apportioned: six months with oil of myrrh, and six months with perfumes and preparations for beautifying women. Thus prepared, each young woman went to the king, and she was given whatever she desired to take with her from the women's quarters to the king's palace. In the evening she went, and in the morning she returned to the second house of the women, to the custody of Shaashgaz, the king's eunuch who kept the concubines. She would not go in to the king again unless the king delighted in her and called for her by name.

Now when the turn came for Esther the daughter of Abihail the uncle of Mordecai, who had taken her as his daughter, to go in to the king, she requested nothing but what Hegai the king's eunuch, the custodian of the women, advised. And Esther obtained favor in the sight of all who saw her.

Having watched over Esther for most of her young life, perhaps we can imagine the anxiety Mordecai may have felt. Where was Esther? How was she being treated? Had she been careful not to reveal her ethnicity? Can you see him pacing? Back and forth. He couldn't enter the women's quarters, but he could hope to catch a glimpse of his dear girl. Was she safe? Was she afraid? What had become of her? Did she know he was there? Mordecai went every day in an attempt to learn anything he could about Esther. I wonder if he ever had any news. What a trial that must have been. What could he do? Mordecai had to trust God with Esther's future.

Have you experienced a situation you couldn't change and had to trust God to take care of someone you loved? What did you do? Being available when they reach out to you for help and covering them in prayer are two things you can do. Reading of Mordecai pacing in the courtyard, I can imagine his silent prayers. He had to rely on God to take care of Esther.

The process of preparing to go to the king took twelve long months. Imagine that! Some women take a lot of time getting ready, but this was preparation intensified! Six months of myrrh, followed by six months of perfumes and beauty treatments—that must have been some salon! I wonder if part of the preparation was learning manners and protocol for approaching the king. Maybe they had classes in etiquette and other cultural expectations.

Looming before these young women was a beauty contest with enormous stakes. This contest changed a woman's life forever. It changed her family's life forever. If she were to win, she would become queen.

If she were to lose, she would be part of the king's harem for the rest of her days. Each young woman had only one opportunity to make an impression, and they were encouraged to make an impression the king wouldn't likely forget. Each could choose clothing, jewelry, headdress, fragrance, make-up—anything to make them the most exotically beautiful of all.

Daily, each woman watched as another had her opportunity. Every morning, a young woman would be returned to the harem. As she returned, she took on the title of concubine. She would not see the king again unless the king **delighted in her and called for her by name.**

Unless invited, she would never see the king again.

The day had finally come. It was Esther's turn. She did not rely on her own wisdom to get ready. She followed Hegai's advice. This reveals a humble, wise, and teachable spirit. As Hegai coached her and helped her dress, she must have listened carefully to his every word. She requested only whatever Hegai advised.

Esther obtained favor in the sight of all who saw her. Beautiful in form and face. She must have been stunning.

"People judge by outward appearance, but the Lord looks at the heart."
1 Samuel 16:7

...six months with oil of myrrh, and six months with perfumes and preparations for beautifying women.

"She is clothed with strength and dignity, and she laughs without fear of the future. When she speaks, her words are wise, and she gives instructions with kindness."

Proverbs 31:25-26

Esther, undercover daughter of the Most High God, was led into the palace of the king.

My Treasure From God's Word...

_____

_____

_____

_____

_____

_____

_____

_____

_____

_____

_____

_____

_____

_____

_____

_____

_____

_____

_____

_____

_____

_____

"Don't be afraid, for I am with you. Don't be discouraged, for I am your God. I will strengthen you and help you. I will hold you up with my victorious right hand." Isaiah 41:10

Favor

To gain a better understanding, we will take a little side-road.   We will focus on the word *favor*. Another word for favor is *grace*. It is unmerited favor. Something that cannot be earned. Let's look at several instances in scripture where we read that someone found or obtained favor.

We will start with Noah.

> *"The LORD observed the extent of human wickedness on the earth, and he saw that everything they thought or imagined was consistently and totally evil. So the LORD was sorry he had ever made them and put them on the earth. It broke his heart. And the LORD said, "I will wipe this human race I have created from the face of the earth. Yes, and I will destroy every living thing—all the people, the large animals, the small animals that scurry along the ground, and even the birds of the sky. I am sorry I ever made them." But Noah found favor with the LORD. This is the account of Noah and his family. Noah was a righteous man, the only blameless person living on earth at the time, and he walked in close fellowship with God."*
> Genesis 6:5-9

Please note that **Noah found favor with God**. Scripture states this point about Noah before it mentions that he was a righteous man, a blameless person, who walked in close fellowship with God. God's favor, or grace, does not depend on who we are or what we do. It depends on His great love.

Let's move on to Joseph.

> *"So Joseph found favor in his sight, and served him. Then he made him overseer of his house, and all that he had he put under his authority."*
> Genesis 39:4 NKJV

Having been sold into slavery by his brothers, Joseph is purchased by Potiphar. In time, he **found favor** in Potiphar's sight and was given more responsibility and authority.

"But the LORD was with Joseph and showed him mercy, and He gave him favor in the sight of the keeper of the prison. And the keeper of the prison committed to Joseph's hand all the prisoners who were in the prison; whatever they did there, it was his doing." Genesis 39:21 NKJV

"The keeper of the prison did not look into anything that was under Joseph's authority, because the LORD was with him; and whatever he did, the Lord made it prosper." Genesis 39:23 NKJV

Look where the favor or grace comes from in this instance. It is from God. God gives favor to whomever He will, and in this case, Joseph was **given favor** in the sight of the keeper of the prison. Why? Because the Lord was with him and prospered him in everything he did.

"And the patriarchs, becoming envious, sold Joseph into Egypt. But God was with him and delivered him out of all his troubles, and gave him favor and wisdom in the presence of Pharaoh, king of Egypt; and he made him governor over Egypt and all his house." Acts 7:9-10 NKJV

"And Pharaoh said to his servants, "Can we find such a one as this, a man in whom is the Spirit of God?" Genesis 41:38 NKJV

Joseph was **given favor** with men by God. It is grace. A gift. A gift of God's love.

There are many other examples of God's favor to man throughout His Word, but we will close this chapter with just one more.

You and me.

"Even before he made the world, God loved us and chose us in Christ to be holy and without fault in his eyes. God decided in advance to adopt us into his own family by bringing us to himself through Jesus Christ. This is what he wanted to do, and it gave him great pleasure. So we praise God for the glorious grace he has poured out on us who belong to his dear Son." Ephesians 1:3-6

When God our Savior
revealed his kindness and
love, he saved us, not because
of the righteous things we
had done, but because of his
mercy. Titus 3:4-5

"God <u>saved you by his grace</u> when you believed. And you can't take credit for this; <u>it is a gift from God</u>. Salvation is not a reward for the good things we have done, so none of us can boast about it."

Ephesians 2:8-9

"All praise to God, the Father of our Lord Jesus Christ. It is <u>by his great mercy</u> that we have been born again, because God raised Jesus Christ from the dead. Now we live with great expectation, and <u>we have a priceless inheritance</u>—an inheritance that is kept in heaven for you, pure and undefiled, beyond the reach of change and decay. And through your faith, God is protecting you by his power until you receive this salvation, which is ready to be revealed on the last day for all to see."

1 Peter 1:3-5

You see, friend, favor is a gift. Something we cannot earn. **But why would God direct His favor toward any of us?**

God's favor, also called **grace,** demonstrates His love and is a gift freely offered to all people through the death, burial, and resurrection of His Son, Jesus. When we accept God's free gift, we become heirs with Christ.

How do we accept God's gift of grace?

It is by our choosing to **believe** that God has set His favor upon us, that He loves us, and that because of His love, He sent Jesus to pay the penalty for our sin. We chose faith, believing that Jesus died, was buried, and was raised again to life, for our justification. This is how we accept God's gift of grace. By faith. Jesus came for this very purpose.

"When we were utterly helpless, Christ came at just the right time and died for us sinners. Now, most people would not be willing to die for an upright person, though someone might perhaps be willing to die for a person who is especially good. But God showed his great love for us by sending Christ to die for us while we were still sinners. And since we have been made right in God's sight by the blood of Christ, he will certainly save us from God's condemnation. For since our friendship with God was restored by the death of his Son while we were still his enemies, we will certainly be saved through

the life of his Son. So now we can rejoice in our wonderful new relationship with God because our Lord Jesus Christ has made us friends of God."   Romans 5:6-11

God sent Jesus to die so that you and I might live. Esther's story is a foreshadow of this wonderful truth.

God has been in the grace-giving business from the beginning. We have looked at only a few examples. There are many! His favor to Noah preserved a remnant of the human race. His favor to Joseph saved the world (especially the Jews) from famine. The favor we observe in the life of Esther is yet another way God preserved His people. We learn from their stories that God is always at work behind the scenes, working for our good.

Through each of those stories, God's promise of redemption was preserved. They were leading up to the ultimate favor of all, the blessing of His Son. Jesus is God's gift of love to the world. He is the way of redemption. God's favor toward you and me is found in Jesus.

   "The Father sent His Son to be the Savior of the world." 1 John 4:14.

What have you learned about God's grace today? How has this understanding impacted you?

Write about it here. This is a good time to think about all the ways God has favored you. Thank Him that He kept His promise of redemption by sending His dear Son and has made it available to you.

My Treasure From God's Word...

_____

_____

_____

_____

_____

_____

_____

_____

_____

_____

_____

_____

_____

_____

"God saved you by his grace when you believed. And you can't take credit for this; it is a gift from God. Salvation is not a reward for the good things we have done, so none of us can boast about it." Ephesians 2:8-9

Chosen

Read: Esther 2:16-23

Esther was taken to King Xerxes at the royal palace in early winter of the seventh year of his reign. And the king loved Esther more than any of the other young women. He was so delighted with her that he set the royal crown on her head and declared her queen instead of Vashti. To celebrate the occasion, he gave a great banquet in Esther's honor for all his nobles and officials, declaring a public holiday for the provinces and giving generous gifts to everyone.

Even after all the young women had been transferred to the second harem and Mordecai had become a palace official, Esther continued to keep her family background and nationality a secret. She was still following Mordecai's directions, just as she did when she lived in his home.

One day as Mordecai was on duty at the king's gate, two of the king's eunuchs, Bigthana and Teresh—who were guards at the door of the king's private quarters—became angry at King Xerxes and plotted to assassinate him. But Mordecai heard about the plot and gave the information to Queen Esther. She then told the king about it and gave Mordecai credit for the report. When an investigation was made and Mordecai's story was found to be true, the two men were impaled on a sharpened pole. This was all recorded in The Book of the History of King Xerxes' Reign.

Of all the young women in his harem, Xerxes chose Esther! He made her his queen. He set the royal crown on her head, then declared another celebration! Known as the **Feast of Esther,** all the important people were invited, but this time it was to *honor* the queen. If that wasn't enough, the celebration was also declared a public holiday in all the provinces, and gifts were given to everyone.

We aren't told what kind of start Vashti had when she became queen, but Esther's coronation is certainly one to ponder. Xerxes, still unaware of her ethnicity, made young Esther, a Jewess, queen of the Persian empire. The crown being a symbol, her becoming queen meant actual marriage to the king. Esther became royalty by marriage.

And the king loved Esther
more than any of the
other women.

This is a beautiful parallel to the church as the Bride of Christ.

♦ Just as Xerxes shared his joy over his new queen with all of Persia, God and all of heaven rejoice over us when we put our faith in Him (Luke 15).

♦ Generous gifts were given to everyone from the king's bounty. As believers, we have every spiritual blessing, but it is not out of God's bounty. It is so much more! It is ***"according to His riches in glory in Christ Jesus"***! Philippians 4:19 NASB. Nothing is held back! God's blessings to His bride befit His glory, His ability, and the vastness of His riches. ***"The earth is the Lord's and everything in it…"*** Psalm 24:1. Friend, if you know Jesus, you have it all!

♦ Before becoming queen, Esther was orphaned, exiled, and captive. As queen, she was royal, honored, and respected. She took on a new identity. She was a wife, the bride of King Xerxes.

♦ Before coming to Christ, we are condemned, enslaved to sin, and spiritually dead. As the Bride of Christ, we are forgiven, walking in freedom, and spiritually alive. We take on a new identity. We are His church, the Bride of Christ.

As we near the end of the scripture reading for today, we read that Mordecai was **on duty at the king's gate.** This would have been a place where important transactions and official business took place. Mordecai was something like an advisor or an elder. Respected. Maybe Esther had used her influence to promote her cousin. We are not told, but what we do observe is that Mordecai was not power-hungry. We don't read of his trying to cash-in on his relationship with Esther. We don't see him grabbing for riches, position, or fame as some men would have done. Mordecai was a faithful man whose life demonstrated integrity and loyalty.

One day, Mordecai overheard two disgruntled men, who were guards at the king's private quarters, planning to assassinate the king. If the assassination attempt had been successful, Esther might have been free to leave the palace. I wonder if Mordecai considered that. He could have kept this information to himself, but like his ancestor, Joseph (Genesis 41–50), he chose loyalty to the king. God used Mordecai's faith, integrity, and loyalty as a link in a chain of events that would, in time, bring about the salvation of all Jewish people throughout the Persian Empire.

Mordecai was in the right place at the right time, doing the right thing. By telling Esther of the assassination plot, the news went straight to the king. Before long, the would-be assassins were hanged. As was done in those days, these events were recorded in the king's chronicles, and although Esther gave Mordecai credit for warning the king, Mordecai was not honored or rewarded. But as we have noted before, Mordecai didn't seem to be seeking recognition. As a man of integrity, he seemed content doing what was right.

"And we know [with great confidence] that God [who is deeply concerned about us] causes all things to work together [as a plan] for good for those who love God, to those who are called according to His plan and purpose." Romans 8:28 AMP

"Second causes (such as people or circumstances) are powerless to act except by God's permission; and what He permits becomes really His arranging." —Hannah Whitall Smith

"The steps of a man are established by the LORD, when he delights in his way." Psalm 37:23 ESV

Mordecai was on duty at the king's gate...

Can you put yourself into the story? Take time to imagine Esther's emotions, her thoughts, and the ramifications of her new identity as queen. Did she wonder what God was doing? How did she feel about hiding her ethnicity and her faith? How about Mordecai? How had life changed for him? His loyalty was not acknowledged. How do you think he felt? Has something like this happened to you? What did you do? Did you choose to trust God?

My Treasure From God's Word...

_____

_____

_____

_____

_____

_____

_____

_____

_____

_____

_____

_____

_____

_____

_____

_____

_____

_____

_____

_____

_____

"Never let loyalty and kindness leave you! Tie them around your neck as a reminder. Write them deep within your heart. Then you will find favor with both God and people, and you will earn a good reputation." Proverbs 3:3-4

Promotion

Read: Esther 3:1-6

> *Some time later King Xerxes promoted Haman son of Hammedatha the Agagite over all the other nobles, making him the most powerful official in the empire. All the king's officials would bow down before Haman to show him respect whenever he passed by, for so the king had commanded. But Mordecai refused to bow down or show him respect.*
>
> *Then the palace officials at the king's gate asked Mordecai, "Why are you disobeying the king's command?" They spoke to him day after day, but still he refused to comply with the order. So they spoke to Haman about this to see if he would tolerate Mordecai's conduct, since Mordecai had told them he was a Jew.*
>
> *When Haman saw that Mordecai would not bow down or show him respect, he was filled with rage. He had learned of Mordecai's nationality, so he decided it was not enough to lay hands on Mordecai alone. Instead, he looked for a way to destroy all the Jews throughout the entire empire of Xerxes.*

Wait! What happened? Shouldn't Mordecai have been awarded a promotion? He saved the king's life! But this promotion was not for loyal, heroic **Mordecai, the Jew**. This promotion was for **Haman, the Agagite**. He is new to our story, and to understand the significance of Haman, we need a bit of history.

Many years prior, as Israel (the Jews) journeyed out of Egypt, the Amalekites attacked them. They came unprovoked against the stragglers, the sick, and the old. Having no water and coming fresh out of slavery, the people of Israel had no weapons and no way to defend themselves. By this act, the Amalekites demonstrated no fear of God (Deuteronomy 25:17–19). Moses, being the leader of Israel, went to God in prayer and, in time, directed Israel to go to battle with the Amalekites. Their leader, Amalek, was killed, and a great victory was won.

"Then the LORD said to Moses, "Write this in a book as a memorial and recite it to Joshua, that I will utterly blot out the memory of Amalek from under heaven." Moses built an altar and named it The LORD is My Banner; and he said, "The LORD has sworn; the LORD will have war against Amalek from generation to generation." Exodus 17:14-16

This was God's edict. His unchangeable, irreversible judgment against the Amalekites.

Another four hundred years passed. Israel rejected God's plan to be their only king. They wanted a man, so God gave them their first king, Saul. Through the prophet Samuel, God told Saul that it was time for judgment to come to the people of Amalek. God told Israel to utterly destroy everyone and everything belonging to the Amalekites. Saul and his men carried out the Lord's command, but only partially. Saul thought he knew more than God. *"Saul and his men spared Agag's life and kept the best of the sheep and goats, the cattle, the fat calves, and the lambs—everything, in fact, that appealed to them. They destroyed only what was worthless or of poor quality."* 1 Samuel 15:9. Because Saul didn't fully obey the Lord, some descendants of King Agag lived. This brings us to the book of Esther, and who should we discover as the enemy of the Jews? *Haman, the Agagite. Descendant of Agag, the King of the Amalekites.* Hatred and anger had been passed down through the generations!

You see, friend, as you read through scripture or hear a story from the Bible, it may seem that these stories are disconnected, that each story stands on its own, separate from the others. But that is not the case. These are not a series of unrelated stories. They are all connected in some way, and they are all working together to lead us to the larger, more important story: God's plan of redemption for all men by the death, burial, and resurrection of the Lord Jesus Christ. God had a plan. God always has a plan. God is good. He is always working for our good.

We are not told how it came about, but King Xerxes decided to promote *Haman.* Rising in power and influence, Haman became the most powerful official in all of the empire. Even the other officials were required to bow to Haman. This was the king's command. Every time Haman came around, Mordecai refused to bow. How could he bow to an Agagite, the enemy of

King Xerxes promoted Haman...the Agagite.

the God of Israel, the enemy of his people? Mordecai was faced with a choice. Bow, or face the consequences. He decided to side with God and his people. So, it was that this is how Mordecai revealed himself as a Jew. It seems that the other officials tried to convince him of the repercussions of not obeying the king's order, but Mordecai decided that in this case, it was more important to side with God than with men.

Have you ever had to make a difficult choice such as this? The Bible teaches us to obey and submit to the civil authorities over us. All authority comes from God. The authorities are God's servants sent for our good (Romans 13). Yet we know there are and will be circumstances in which we have to choose to obey God rather than men (Daniel chapters 3 and 6). Think about Acts chapter 5, when the apostles refused to stop witnessing in Jerusalem, declaring, *"We must obey God rather than men."* In siding with God, Mordecai was in good company! Mordecai refused to bow to Haman the Agagite.

Noticing that Mordecai refused to bow to him, Haman was enraged. He couldn't handle it that one man would not bow down. Haman was all about himself. He was a prideful and angry man. This didn't sit well with his ego.

The *helpful* officials let it leak to Haman that Mordecai was a Jew. They seem to wonder if this fact would excuse Mordecai from bowing. I wonder if they had any idea where this information would lead. When he learned that Mordecai was his enemy, Haman decided that punishing Mordecai was not enough. Instead, he would use his position and power to come up with a scheme to annihilate the entire Jewish nation.

A worthless person, a wicked man,
Is the one who walks with a perverse mouth,
Who winks with his eyes, who signals with his feet,
Who points with his fingers;
Who with perversity in his heart continually devises evil,
Who spreads strife.
Therefore his calamity will come suddenly;
Instantly he will be broken and there will be no healing.

There are six things which the LORD hates,
Yes, seven which are an abomination to Him:
Haughty eyes, a lying tongue,

And hands that shed innocent blood,
A heart that devises wicked plans,
Feet that run rapidly to evil,
A false witness who utters lies,
And one who spreads strife among brothers.

Proverbs 6:12-19 NASB

What would you do if you were in Mordecai's position? If the law requires that you *bow down* to something that violates God's law, what will you do? These can be hard questions. There are no easy answers, but it is good to think about the possibility and predetermine in our hearts who we will obey. As the apostles did in **The Book of Acts**, we each must decide for ourselves that we will obey God rather than man and then trust that God is behind the scenes working in ways we cannot see. Just as He was in the story of Mordecai and Esther. Our God is sovereign over all.

My Treasure From God's Word...

_____

_____

_____

_____

_____

_____

_____

_____

_____

_____

_____

_____

_____

_____

_____

_____

_____

_____

"For he is the living God, and he will endure forever. His kingdom will never be destroyed, and his rule will never end. He rescues and saves his people; he performs miraculous signs and wonders in the heavens and on earth. He has rescued Daniel from the power of the lions." Daniel 6:26-27

Part 2

The Edict

"Will God Make a Way?"

"...all Jews—young and old,
including women and children—
must be killed, slaughtered, and
annihilated on a single day."

Esther 3:13

Haman's Plan

Read: Esther 3:7-15

So in the month of April, during the twelfth year of King Xerxes' reign, lots were cast in Haman's presence (the lots were called purim) to determine the best day and month to take action. And the day selected was March 7, nearly a year later.

Then Haman approached King Xerxes and said, "There is a certain race of people scattered through all the provinces of your empire who keep themselves separate from everyone else. Their laws are different from those of any other people, and they refuse to obey the laws of the king. So it is not in the king's interest to let them live. If it please the king, issue a decree that they be destroyed, and I will give 10,000 large sacks of silver to the government administrators to be deposited in the royal treasury."

The king agreed, confirming his decision by removing his signet ring from his finger and giving it to Haman son of Hammedatha the Agagite, the enemy of the Jews. The king said, "The money and the people are both yours to do with as you see fit."

So on April 17 the king's secretaries were summoned, and a decree was written exactly as Haman dictated. It was sent to the king's highest officers, the governors of the respective provinces, and the nobles of each province in their own scripts and languages. The decree was written in the name of King Xerxes and sealed with the king's signet ring. Dispatches were sent by swift messengers into all the provinces of the empire, giving the order that all Jews—young and old, including women and children—must be killed, slaughtered, and annihilated on a single day. This was scheduled to happen on March 7 of the next year. The property of the Jews would be given to those who killed them.

A copy of this decree was to be issued as law in every province and proclaimed to all peoples, so that they would be ready to do their duty on the appointed day. At the king's command, the decree went out by swift messengers, and it was also proclaimed in the fortress

of Susa. Then the king and Haman sat down to drink, but the city of Susa fell into confusion.

Seeking direction, Haman consulted his gods. It seemed he had risen to power by trusting his gods. The casting of lots was a form of astrology, and important decisions required consulting the stars. The casting of lots led Haman to choose March 7th. That was to be the day for the annihilation of the Jews. Being almost a year away must have frustrated Haman, but he would wait. The outcome of lots, even this, was determined by God. It gave the Jews an advantage, allowing them time to prepare and gave Mordecai and Esther time to act.

Haman didn't know it, but the God of the Jews is sovereign over all! It is God who places authority on whomever He will. In Romans 9:17, we read that God told Pharaoh, *"I have appointed you for the very purpose of displaying my power in you and to spread my fame throughout the earth."* And it is God who arranges the timing of it all. *"We may throw the dice, but the Lord determines how they fall."* Proverbs 16:33. Using dice, God told Haman to wait!

Appealing to Xerxes ego, Haman presented his problem and plan to the king. He stated that these were people who had their own laws and, therefore, broke the laws of the land. He didn't even give those *lawbreaking* people a name, but he said they were everywhere throughout the kingdom. They disobey the law of Xerxes, and something must be done to get rid of them. Haman even offered the king a huge sum of money to get rid of these people.

What Xerxes did next is outrageous. He didn't investigate Haman's story. He didn't ask who these people were. He didn't even consult with his wise men. These were things he had previously done when he learned of his assassination attempt. Instead, Xerxes gave Haman his royal signet ring (authority to act in the king's name) and told him to write an edict (an irreversible, unalterable, and irrevocable law) and seal it with the ring. He said, "The money and people are yours. Do with them as you please." This placed the Jews' fate in the hands of this sadistic, egotistical, evil man, Haman.

Immediately, the edict was written. Haman didn't waste any time. It was written in the name of King Xerxes and sealed with his royal signet ring. The edict was written. Set in stone. Copies were sent out to every noble, every

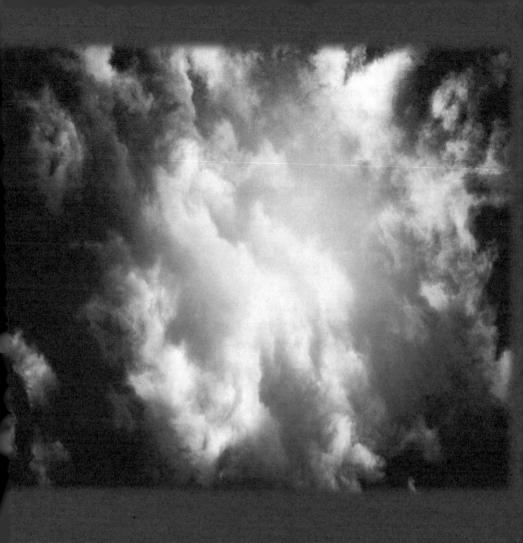

There is a certain race of people

scattered through all the provinces of your empire...

they refuse to obey the laws of the king.

So it is not in the king's interest to let them live.

—Haman

official, and every province in every language. Haman sought to make sure that everyone and anyone would be able to understand this new law. His law. On March 7th of the following year, every Jew, including women and children, was to be destroyed, killed, and annihilated in a single day, and all of their belongings would belong to those who killed them. I guess Haman reasoned that this was an incentive to get the job done. Haman was passing judgment to eliminate and exterminate an entire nation. However, he was on a slippery slope, because judgment belongs to God.

The passage ends with Xerxes and Haman sitting at a table and having a drink together. While they were behaving as though it were any other day, the people of Susa were in confusion.

They must have questioned how and why all of this came about. Was there a way of escape for the Jews? It may have seemed hopeless, but our sovereign God had two people already in place—Mordecai and Esther. He was ready to act on behalf of His people.

My Treasure From God's Word...

_____

_____

_____

_____

_____

_____

_____

_____

_____

_____

_____

_____

_____

_____

_____

_____

_____

_____

"My help comes from the Lord who made heaven and earth!
He will not let you stumble; the one who watches over you
will not slumber. Indeed, He who watches over Israel will
not slumber or sleep." Psalm 121:2-4

Mordecai's Mourning

Read: Esther 4:1-9

When Mordecai learned about all that had been done, he tore his clothes, put on burlap and ashes, and went out into the city, crying with a loud and bitter wail. He went as far as the gate of the palace, for no one was allowed to enter the palace gate while wearing clothes of mourning. And as news of the king's decree reached all the provinces, there was great mourning among the Jews. They fasted, wept, and wailed, and many people lay in burlap and ashes.

When Queen Esther's maids and eunuchs came and told her about Mordecai, she was deeply distressed. She sent clothing to him to replace the burlap, but he refused it. Then Esther sent for Hathach, one of the king's eunuchs who had been appointed as her attendant. She ordered him to go to Mordecai and find out what was troubling him and why he was in mourning. So Hathach went out to Mordecai in the square in front of the palace gate.

Mordecai told him the whole story, including the exact amount of money Haman had promised to pay into the royal treasury for the destruction of the Jews. Mordecai gave Hathach a copy of the decree issued in Susa that called for the death of all Jews. He asked Hathach to show it to Esther and explain the situation to her. He also asked Hathach to direct her to go to the king to beg for mercy and plead for her people. So Hathach returned to Esther with Mordecai's message.

While the previous scene closed with Xerxes and Haman enjoying a drink as though all was well, this one opens with Mordecai and his people in great grief and mourning. For them, everything had changed. All of the city was in confusion; the Jews were facing extermination, and those within the palace walls were oblivious to it all.

Mordecai tore his clothes (an expression of grief), put on sackcloth (purposefully irritating clothes that signify mourning), poured ashes over himself (a sign of repentance), and loudly and bitterly cried out as he sat by the king's gate and walked through the city. Jews everywhere did the same.

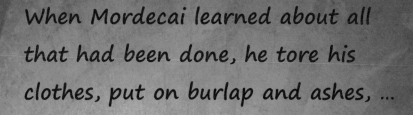

When Mordecai learned about all that had been done, he tore his clothes, put on burlap and ashes, ...

He went as far as the gate of the palace, for no one was allowed to enter the palace gate while wearing clothes of mourning.

As Mordecai made his way back to the palace, he stopped at the king's gate. People in mourning were not permitted entry. The royalty lived in a protected and sheltered world. No unpleasantness was allowed. There was to be nothing negative to affect the king's mood. So, Queen Esther was unaware of the evil plan that Haman had put into motion. It was already a law. An unalterable, irrevocable law that the king himself could not change.

Some of Queen Esther's servants heard of Mordecai's sad condition and reported it to her. She cared for her cousin and must have wondered what was so terribly wrong. The fact of his mournful condition deeply distressed her. It seems strange that she didn't immediately try to find out the source of Mordecai's anguish, but perhaps she was being cautious in questioning him as she had to communicate with him by way of servants who likely didn't know that they were Jews or that they were even related. Thinking she could perhaps be a comfort to her cousin, Esther sent new clothes for him, but Mordecai refused them. The irritating sackcloth helped him to be mindful of his anguish and intentional in seeking God's help. The ashes signified his state of humility before God and repentance of sin.

Did he feel responsible for this change of events? I wonder if he thought that if he had just bowed down and kept quiet about his ethnicity and faith, this would not have come about. His loud crying and wailing was a spectacle that drew attention to what was coming for his people. Through this, he clearly identified himself with his people, the Jews. Mordecai, the respected advisor, was a Jew!

When Esther learned that he refused the change of clothes and, therefore, a change of heart, she sent her servant, the eunuch Hathach, to inquire why. What had happened? Why was Mordecai so distressed? With business dealings, court proceedings, official meetings and all the hustle and bustle of the courtyard, the servant found Mordecai still in mourning and sitting by the king's gate. At Esther's request, Mordecai recounted all the details to her servant.

He explained how it began with the king's command that all should bow to **Haman the Agagite.** He stated that he, Mordecai, refused to bow to God's enemy. Esther would have known of Israel's history with regard to the

Mordecai commanded the queen to go before the king, pleading for mercy and begging for the lives of her people.

Agagites. Mordecai further explained that his refusal to bow to wicked Haman brought out the secret of their heritage, and those two facts stirred up indignation, pride, anger, and a plan for revenge in the heart of their enemy. He spoke of Haman's offer to pay a large sum of money to the king's treasury in exchange for the destruction of the Jews. Mordecai then gave the servant a copy of the edict so that Esther could read it for herself. Esther was to show it to the king since Mordecai could not enter the gate. She was to explain the situation. Mordecai then commanded the queen to go before the king, pleading for mercy and begging for the lives of her people. **Mordecai commanded the queen.** The servant returned to Queen Esther and told her all his words.

My Treasure From God's Word...

_____

_____

_____

_____

_____

_____

_____

_____

_____

_____

_____

_____

_____

_____

_____

_____

_____

_____

_____

_____

"Even when I walk through the darkest valley, I will not be afraid, for you are close beside me. Your rod and your staff protect and comfort me." Psalm 23:4

Esther's Choice

Read: Esther 4:10-17

Then Esther told Hathach to go back and relay this message to Mordecai: "All the king's officials and even the people in the provinces know that anyone who appears before the king in his inner court without being invited is doomed to die unless the king holds out his gold scepter. And the king has not called for me to come to him for thirty days." So Hathach gave Esther's message to Mordecai.

Mordecai sent this reply to Esther: "Don't think for a moment that because you're in the palace you will escape when all other Jews are killed. If you keep quiet at a time like this, deliverance and relief for the Jews will arise from some other place, but you and your relatives will die. Who knows if perhaps you were made queen for just such a time as this?"

Then Esther sent this reply to Mordecai: "Go and gather together all the Jews of Susa and fast for me. Do not eat or drink for three days, night or day. My maids and I will do the same. And then, though it is against the law, I will go in to see the king. If I must die, I must die." So Mordecai went away and did everything as Esther had ordered him.

Fear and impossibility must have taken a grip on Queen Esther's young heart! In her response to Mordecai, she states the facts: Going before the king uninvited was suicide! Xerxes had not called her for thirty days. Knowing the king's big ego and that he would go to great lengths to protect his pride, approaching him uninvited would be against all wisdom and sensibility. It just shouldn't be done!

The last words of Mordecai's response to her are perhaps the passage that readers are most familiar with. Mordecai told it to her straight. She shouldn't fool herself into thinking that she would be protected because she was queen. She was a Jew, and that would be found out. If she didn't make an attempt to save her people, help would come some other way, but being his cousin, they both would be killed. That is followed by those well-known words:

***Who knows if perhaps you were made queen for just such a time
as this?***

What words! Is it a wonder they are often spoken and often repeated?
From the time of Esther to this very day, by those same words, believers
have been encouraged, challenged, and strengthened to do whatever God
has called them to do.

Perhaps God has brought you to _____ for such a time as this.

Perhaps God has allowed _____ in your life for such a time as this.

Perhaps God gave you _____ for such a time as this.

Have you ever come to a time when you had to consider, "Is
this_____ for such a time as this?" Just like Esther, there are times
when you and I have choices to make. Will we trust God? When we cannot
see His hand, will we trust His heart? Will we believe all His promises to be
true? Do we believe that He is always working for our good and that He is
only good? Will we step into the unknown when God shows us the way?

Mordecai told Esther that if she chose to protect herself by keeping silent,
help would come another way. What faith! Have you noticed in your reading that the name of God is never mentioned once in ***The Book of Esther***?
Yet, the work and wonderful activity of God are evident to all who believe.

**"Just because you can't see the air, doesn't mean you stop breathing.
And just because you can't see God, doesn't mean you stop believing."**
—Nicky Gumbel

We know that God loves the Jewish people. We know that God commanded the destruction of the Amalekites as enemies of His people. We know
that King Saul disobeyed God by allowing Agag, the Amalekite, to live. And
we know that **God had sworn that he would be at war with Amalek from
generation to generation. God said he would erase the memory of Amalek from under heaven.** This was God's edict. An irreversible, unchangeable judgment against the descendants of Amalek. Lastly, we know that
Haman was a descendant of Agag and a sworn enemy of the Jews. Queen
Esther knew it too.

Growing up, the child, Esther, would have heard many of the stories of her people, Israel, running to the Lord, their God, for deliverance from their enemies. She also likely knew many of the Psalms of David. Maybe she immediately began reminding herself that her help comes from the Lord, the Maker of heaven and earth.

> **"The secret of survival in enemy territory? Remember…**
> **Remember what God has already done." —**Max Lucado

The young Queen Esther had a choice to make. But where was God? How could this be His plan? What of all the promises of faithful protection, deliverance, and blessings? What of the Promised One who would come to the world through the Jews? Could God's plan be thwarted? What could *she* do? What *should* she do? Was God giving her a chance to save her people?

Esther ran to God in prayer. In fact, she led her people throughout Persia to seek God's help through prayer and fasting.

> *"Therefore, let all the godly pray to you while there is still time,*
> *that they may not drown in the floodwaters of judgment.*
> *For you are my hiding place; you protect me from trouble.*
> *You surround me with songs of victory."* Psalm 32:6-7

Now, the Bible doesn't say *prayer and fasting*, but the understanding is clear. You see, in biblical fasting, the focus is not solely on the withholding of food or drink. It is a spiritual practice and includes prayer. All through the Bible, people can be found fasting to show repentance, to express grief, or to ask for help with such things as guidance, protection, humility, ministry, temptation, and even worship. It is a spiritual focus and is always coupled with prayer. By telling Mordecai that all the Jews of Persia should join with her and the servants in fasting for three days and three nights, Esther was calling for prayer!

Now, if it were me, I would have called for prayer so that I would *know what to do*. But Esther already knew what she had to do. I think her call for prayer was *to prepare her heart for what God had chosen her to do and to beg God to intervene on behalf of the Jews*. Queen Esther was given a chance and a choice. Like Jesus, she had been called to "lay down" her life for her *friends*.

Then Esther sent this reply to Mordecai: "Go and gather together all the Jews of Susa and fast for me. Do not eat or drink for three days, night or day. My maids and I will do the same. And then, though it is against the law,

I will go in to see the king.
If I must die, I must die."

"The wonderful thing about praying is that you leave a world of not being able to do something, and enter God's realm where everything is possible. Nothing is too great for his almighty power. Nothing is too small for His love." —Corrie Ten Boom

"There is no greater love than to lay down one's life for one's friends."
John 15:13

My Treasure From God's Word...

_____

_____

_____

_____

_____

_____

_____

_____

_____

_____

_____

_____

_____

_____

_____

_____

_____

_____

_____

_____

"The LORD is my light and my salvation—so why should I be afraid? The LORD is my fortress, protecting me from danger, so why should I tremble?" Psalm 27:1

Esther's Chance

Read: Esther 5:1-8

On the third day of the fast, Esther put on her royal robes and entered the inner court of the palace, just across from the king's hall. The king was sitting on his royal throne, facing the entrance. When he saw Queen Esther standing there in the inner court, he welcomed her and held out the gold scepter to her. So Esther approached and touched the end of the scepter.

Then the king asked her, "What do you want, Queen Esther? What is your request? I will give it to you, even if it is half the kingdom!"

And Esther replied, "If it please the king, let the king and Haman come today to a banquet I have prepared for the king."

The king turned to his attendants and said, "Tell Haman to come quickly to a banquet, as Esther has requested." So the king and Haman went to Esther's banquet.

And while they were drinking wine, the king said to Esther, "Now tell me what you really want. What is your request? I will give it to you, even if it is half the kingdom!"

Esther replied, "This is my request and deepest wish. If I have found favor with the king, and if it pleases the king to grant my request and do what I ask, please come with Haman tomorrow to the banquet I will prepare for you. Then I will explain what this is all about."

The three days of prayer and fasting had ended. This was Esther's chance. Upon seeing her, what would the king think? It was against the law. What would he feel? He had not called for his queen wife in over thirty days. What would he do? As she approached, would he hold out the golden scepter to her to indicate his approval? Was God going before her to prepare his heart? Only three days prior, just considering this day seemed suicidal. Something that shouldn't be done and couldn't be done. Yet, on this day, having earnestly and completely presented the need to God, we find Esther preparing herself to go, uninvited, into the presence of the king.

Esther put on her royal
robes and entered the inner
court of the palace...

Realizing her higher calling, Esther resolved to risk her life and leave the outcome to God.   There are times in life when each of us must choose to take that step of faith and leave the outcome to God.

"Prayer is putting oneself into the hands of God." —Mother Teresa

"Faith is the bridge between where I am and where God is taking me."
—Unknown

How much faith do we need? Jesus said seemingly impossible things can be accomplished with faith as small as a mustard seed. So, faith may not be the problem. The problem may be that we perceive our God as small. When we perceive God as small, we need a change of perspective. God is sovereign. He is Lord over all. Our true need is not more faith; it is more of God!

By going before the king uninvited, Esther wasn't **taking a chance**. She was **trusting for a chance** to save the Jews. She was trusting her sovereign God to give her favor with the king.

"I will answer them before they even call to me. While they are still talking about their needs, I will go ahead and answer their prayers!"
Isaiah 65:24

"Nothing before, nothing behind; the steps of faith fall on the seeming void, and find the rock beneath." —John Greenleaf Whittier

**"Oh utter but the name of God in your heart of hearts,
And see how from the soul at once all anxious fear departs."**
—Hannah Whitall Smith

So, with her heart prepared, Queen Esther put on her royal robes and entered the inner court. There, she stopped. King Xerxes was on the throne, and from that vantage point, he could see Esther. He welcomed her. What were his thoughts? Did a smile suddenly light up his face for all to see? As he held out the golden scepter, Esther safely approached the throne. She showed gratitude for his favor and submission to his authority as she carefully reached out and touched the tip of the scepter.

It may be challenging for us today to understand the culture and tradition of those days. Especially with regard to relationships and royalty. Everyone, even his wife, lived in submission to the will and whim of the king. It hadn't been Esther's choice to leave all that she knew to live in the palace, forever belonging to the king. But that is where she found herself. Somehow, God was at work in all of it. In both the good and the evil, God would bring about His promise to the Jews. Through all of it, Esther knew her place, and she chose to let God use her to touch the heart of the king.

We know that Xerxes was pleased to see her. We read that he welcomed her approach by asking her what she wanted. How tiresome must it have been that everyone wanted something from the king? He knew well the risk she had taken by coming uninvited. He likely reasoned that she must need something very important from him. His heart was prepared to give her up to half his kingdom! What a relief those words must have been to her heart! She had the king's favor! God had prepared the way.

This could have been her chance. Perhaps this was her one chance to say what she came to say, but in her spirit, God must have nudged her to wait. Instead of presenting her need, she chose another course. Continuing to kneel before the throne, prayerfully and carefully choosing her words, she requested Xerxes and Haman to come to the banquet she had prepared for that very day. The king's interest was stirred. Xerxes immediately sent for Haman to join him for Esther's banquet.

While enjoying the meal and sharing a drink, the king turned to Esther and asked her a second time, "Esther, tell me, what is it that you really want? Tell me, I will give you up to half my kingdom." Esther had stirred his heart, and his curiosity was building. What was this all about? What did she need? He wanted to please her.

Friend, with each mention of Esther being favored, we are witnessing the goodness of God!

Esther replied to the king with her request and it was this: That the king and Haman join her the following day for another banquet. At that time, she would be ready for the king to hear her petition.

Esther postponed her request! The king wasn't accustomed to having to wait. His interest intensified! We have to wonder: *What was her plan?* Did she know how she would present her request the next day? Was it a mystery even to Esther? Other than a banquet, did she know what she would do and say?

What we do know is this: God was with her, and He would make a way. He is known for making a way when there seems to be no way!

"The LORD will guide you continually, giving you water when you are dry and restoring your strength. You will be like a well-watered garden, like an ever-flowing spring." Isaiah 58:11

My Treasure From God's Word...

_____

_____

_____

_____

_____

_____

_____

_____

_____

_____

_____

_____

_____

_____

_____

_____

_____

_____

_____

_____

_____

"The LORD says, "I will rescue those who love me. I will protect those who trust in my name. When they call on me, I will answer; I will be with them in trouble. I will rescue and honor them." Psalm 91:14–15

Haman's Pride

Read: Esther 5:9-14

Haman was a happy man as he left the banquet! But when he saw Mordecai sitting at the palace gate, not standing up or trembling nervously before him, Haman became furious. However, he restrained himself and went on home.

Then Haman gathered together his friends and Zeresh, his wife, and boasted to them about his great wealth and his many children. He bragged about the honors the king had given him and how he had been promoted over all the other nobles and officials.

Then Haman added, "And that's not all! Queen Esther invited only me and the king himself to the banquet she prepared for us. And she has invited me to dine with her and the king again tomorrow!" Then he added, "But this is all worth nothing as long as I see Mordecai the Jew just sitting there at the palace gate."

So Haman's wife, Zeresh, and all his friends suggested, "Set up a *sharpened pole that stands seventy-five feet tall, and in the morning ask the king to impale Mordecai on it. When this is done, you can go on your merry way to the banquet with the king." This pleased Haman, and he ordered the pole set up.

*Some versions refer to this as a *gallows*. From history we know that the Persians often impaled people while alive so they suffered a slow, painful death.

Let's think of this passage as a sort of self-pleased sandwich filled with Haman's pride, slathered with bragging, and a side of loathing. This describes Haman's mindset when he returned home after Esther's first banquet. He left the banquet "happy," then pridefully bragged to his family and friends about his self-declared greatness, which was interrupted with loathing at every thought of Mordecai, the Jew, but once presented with the idea of murdering Mordecai, he went on his way in delight.

He had left the banquet happy. With a glad heart. He had felt very self-important. Then, what happened? As he journeyed home, he saw Mordecai. Mordecai didn't honor him. This Jew wasn't afraid of him. It made his blood boil! Haman restrained himself— perhaps trying to hold on to the euphoria he felt from being honored by a meal alone with the king and queen. His confidence grew as he considered that he was a man of great importance. So, holding back his fury, Haman made his way home. Once home, he began his strut! Gathering his wife and friends, Haman made sure they knew what a great man of importance and honor he had become. He boasted of his great riches, his many children, and the various ways the king had promoted him. He was to be honored above every official and servant of the king! *He had been taken into the king's confidence.* Now, this is the height of his self-magnification: *The queen values me above everyone else. He alone, had been invited to dine with the king and queen!* Likely no one else had ever been given this honor! If that was not enough, this was not a one-time occurrence. He was already invited a second time the next day to dine alone with the king and queen. What an ego trip! How weary his family and friends must have become with all his prideful boasting!

Look at some things the Word of God says about pride.

"Pride ends in humiliation, while humility brings honor." Proverbs 29:23

"The Lord detests the proud; they will surely be punished." Proverbs 16:5

"... I will crush the arrogance of the proud and humble the pride of the mighty." Isaiah 13:11

"...What do you have that God hasn't given you? And if everything you have is from God, why boast as though it were not a gift?"
1 Corinthians 4:7

How does God view this? Remember, pride was the first sin. It is at the top of the *sin list*. It was pride that caused the angel Lucifer to become Satan. Satan used pride to tempt Eve. *"You will be like God."* Genesis 3:5 NIV.

"Pride is the ground in which all other sins grow, and the parent from which all other sins come." —William Barclay, British Bible Scholar

Let's take measures to guard our hearts. Take on the mind of Christ. Who,

Set up a sharpened pole that stands seventy-five feet tall, and in the morning ask the king to impale Mordecai on it.

When this is done you can go on your merry way to your banquet with the king.
—Haman's wife and friends

being God, humbled Himself, dying a criminal's death on the cross for the benefit of those who were yet His enemies. Even those who were not yet born. People such as you and me.

Haman's self-exultation was abruptly interrupted as his mind went back to Mordecai. That infuriating Jew! Mordecai stood in the way of Haman's satisfaction and contentment. As long as he had to look at Mordecai, Haman could not be happy. He was obsessed with Mordecai's defiance. The Jews' annihilation was coming, but not soon enough. What could he do?

His wife and friends likely had enough of his manic behavior as he bounced from over-the-top boasting to utter despair over Mordecai's defiance. They tossed him a solution. Kill Mordecai! Ask the king to have Mordecai impaled for all to see. Haman could then go his way to enjoy time with the king and queen. What an idea! This pleased Haman, so he put the plan into motion.

My Treasure From God's Word...

_____

_____

_____

_____

_____

_____

_____

_____

_____

_____

_____

_____

_____

_____

_____

_____

_____

_____

_____

_____

"The wicked plot against the godly; they snarl at them in defiance. But the Lord just laughs, for he sees their day of judgment coming." Psalm 37:12-13

Haman's Advice

Read: Esther 6:1-9

That night the king had trouble sleeping, so he ordered an attendant to bring the book of the history of his reign so it could be read to him. In those records he discovered an account of how Mordecai had exposed the plot of Bigthana and Teresh, two of the eunuchs who guarded the door to the king's private quarters. They had plotted to assassinate King Xerxes.

"What reward or recognition did we ever give Mordecai for this?" the king asked.

His attendants replied, "Nothing has been done for him."

"Who is that in the outer court?" the king inquired. As it happened, Haman had just arrived in the outer court of the palace to ask the king to impale Mordecai on the pole he had prepared.

So the attendants replied to the king, "Haman is out in the court."

"Bring him in," the king ordered. So Haman came in, and the king said, "What should I do to honor a man who truly pleases me?"

Haman thought to himself, "Whom would the king wish to honor more than me?" So he replied, "If the king wishes to honor someone, he should bring out one of the king's own royal robes, as well as a horse that the king himself has ridden—one with a royal emblem on its head. Let the robes and the horse be handed over to one of the king's most noble officials. And let him see that the man whom the king wishes to honor is dressed in the king's robes and led through the city square on the king's horse. Have the official shout as they go, 'This is what the king does for someone he wishes to honor!'

I find this scene to be tragic, comical, and satisfying. A strange combination, but so reflective of human nature! It is *tragic* in that it shows how completely self-absorbed Haman was. He was blind to anyone else possibly being honored by the king. It also comes at what seems like an inappropriate time because Mordecai, in a spirit of mourning, would be honored. This was likely out of touch with what he perceived to be his current need. It is *comical* because we know Haman was going to dread and abhor what was required of him and *satisfying* because Mordecai was finally being honored for his loyalty to the king! Honored in a big way too! There is hope in this story! But poor Haman! We have got to feel a bit sorry for the guy. He "can't see the forest for the trees!"

Do you see God at work in this story? I hope so! He may not be named, but He is everywhere, working behind the scenes, through both the godless schemes of men and the prayers of His people. God kept and still keeps His promises to the Jews. God's plan for the future cannot be interrupted or intercepted by men. God's plan will always prevail!

"That night the king had trouble sleeping..." I don't intend to imply that trouble sleeping always has a spiritual cause, but in this case, I believe it did! God was behind Xerxes inability to sleep! What can one do when they cannot sleep? Why not read a good book! And what could be more interesting than a book about your own exploits and accomplishments, especially if you are a king? Nothing! So, Xerxes called for a servant to bring the *"book of history of his reign."* Now, I am guessing that some of what was read was mundane, even boring, but one event caught the attention of the king. It was the record of Mordecai's exposure of the plan of Bigthana and Teresh to assassinate the king, yet it said nothing of Mordecai being recognized or rewarded. Upon questioning the servants, Xerxes learned that nothing had been done for this man who demonstrated such loyalty to the king. This should not be! This was outrageous! As king, he publicly rewarded those who were loyal. His lack of doing so was a poor reflection of himself. This had to be made right. With his mind set into motion, Xerxes noticed someone in the outer courts and inquired who it might be. He wanted advice. He would address this oversight today!

Xerxes couldn't wait to reward Mordecai.

"Haman is out in the court," he was told. What was Haman doing in the outer court in the middle of the night when the king would have been expected to still be sleeping? He wanted an early start to the day. Remember what he had planned to request of the king? The execution of Mordecai! He had the pole prepared. This was Haman's hope and expectation.

Haman couldn't wait to kill Mordecai.

The God of the universe had His own plans.

Haman's Wish List

If the king wishes to honor someone, he should bring out one of the king's own royal robes, as well as a horse that the king himself has ridden—one with a royal emblem on its head. Let the robes and the horse be handed over to one of the king's most noble officials. And let him see that the man whom the king wishes to honor is dressed in the king's robes and led through the city square on the king's horse. Have the official shout as they go, 'This is what the king does for someone he wishes to honor!' —Haman

Seeing himself as near to royalty as a non-royal could be, Haman began his detailed suggestions as to how the king should honor the one in whom he delights.

Before we delve into Haman's *wish list*, let's consider the many ways Haman had already been honored. The king had already promoted him in several ways. He had been given authority over all the princes; everyone had to bow down to him; he had access to the king; and he had been entrusted with the king's signet ring. He alone had been invited to dine with the king and queen—twice! But for Haman, this was not enough.

This is human nature. Apart from God, there is no satisfaction. Enough is never enough. This can be observed at the very beginning when God gave Adam and Eve all things to enjoy—everything in the beautiful garden, companionship, dominion over all creation, and daily fellowship with God Himself. Yet they believed Satan's lie that it was not enough. There was only one thing they could not have. The fruit of the Tree of Knowledge of Good and Evil. Their desire for that one thing and disregard for God's law are what changed the course of all mankind. They were not to touch it or eat from it, and they did it anyway. Their sin was not eating a piece of fruit. Their sin was in their disobedience. They were leaning on their own understanding instead of trusting God. They were believing the lie that God was holding back something that they needed. Their sin was seeing themselves on the same level as God! It was pride. (Genesis 2-3)

And then there was Haman. He saw himself on the same level as the king. As that mindset ruined things for Adam and Eve, Haman was on a similar trajectory—*down*. It was and is, to this day, a very slippery slope.

"Trust in the LORD with all your heart; <u>do not depend on your own understanding</u>." Proverbs 3:5

So what did Haman suggest should be done for the man in whom the king delights? He should be given a royal robe. One that has been worn by the king. He should ride a royal horse. One ridden by the king. He should be dressed by the other princes so that he is being served and recognized as superior to them. He should be led through the streets for all to see, and it should be loudly proclaimed, *'This is what the king does for someone he wishes to honor!'*

There is an interesting parallel to honor in the Old Testament. It is the story of Joseph, another Jew. (Genesis 41:40-45)

Joseph didn't seek to be honored, but like Mordecai, he was faithful in his duties, trustworthy in his actions, and earned respect and honor as a man of integrity. The Egyptian Pharoah appointed him ruler over all his house, all his people, and all of Egypt. He was second to Pharaoh in all the land. He was given Pharaoh's signet ring, clothed in fine linen, and a gold chain was put around his neck. He was to ride in the second chariot, and "Bow the knee!" was to be commanded at his approach. Nothing of consequence could be done without Joseph's permission. We have to wonder if Haman knew that story. We can be sure Mordecai did.

Did you know that such honor is yours if you are a child of the Most High God? It is!

We are given a royal robe.

"I am overwhelmed with joy in the LORD my God! For he has dressed me with the clothing of salvation and draped me in a robe of righteousness." Isaiah 61:10

We are sealed (signet ring is a "seal") with the Holy Spirit.

"And when you believed in Christ, he identified you as his own by giving you the Holy Spirit, whom he promised long ago." Ephesians 1:13

We are made part of the royal family.

"So you have not received a spirit that makes you fearful slaves. Instead, you received God's Spirit when he adopted you as his own children. Now we call him, "Abba, Father." For his Spirit joins with our spirit to affirm that we are God's children." Romans 8:15-16

Friend, God identifies Himself with us, dresses us in His righteousness, seals us with His Spirit, and adopts us into His family! There's one more thing. Joseph was given a new name. Look at this.

This is what God says about you if you are a child of God:

"All who are victorious will become pillars in the Temple of my God, and they will never have to leave it. And I will write on them the name of my God, and they will be citizens in the city of my God—the new Jerusalem that comes down from heaven from my God. And I will also write on them my new name." Revelation 3:12

God loves you, and His plan for you is above and beyond anything you have imagined!

My Treasure From God's Word...

_____

_____

_____

_____

_____

_____

_____

_____

_____

_____

_____

_____

_____

_____

_____

_____

_____

_____

_____

_____

_____

_____

_____

"Pride ends in humiliation, while humility brings honor..."
Proverbs 29:23

Haman's Humiliation

Read: Esther 6:10-14

> *"Excellent!" the king said to Haman. "Quick! Take the robes and my horse, and do just as you have said for Mordecai the Jew, who sits at the gate of the palace. Leave out nothing you have suggested!"*
>
> *So Haman took the robes and put them on Mordecai, placed him on the king's own horse, and led him through the city square, shouting, "This is what the king does for someone he wishes to honor!" Afterward Mordecai returned to the palace gate, but Haman hurried home dejected and completely humiliated.*
>
> *When Haman told his wife, Zeresh, and all his friends what had happened, his wise advisers and his wife said, "Since Mordecai—this man who has humiliated you—is of Jewish birth, you will never succeed in your plans against him. It will be fatal to continue opposing him."*
>
> *While they were still talking, the king's eunuchs arrived and quickly took Haman to the banquet Esther had prepared.*

Although we know that God was at work to bring about His plan for the completion of His will and the benefit of His chosen people, it has become even more evident in this part of the story that God was turning the tide for Haman. Although the day began with Haman's excitement and anticipation of eliminating Mordecai, it had taken a very unexpected direction. God had turned the story upside down!

Xerxes was pleased with Haman's advice and commanded him to do just as he had said—every bit of it, and without delay. Who was to be honored? **Mordecai, the Jew**.

"Huh? Excuse me?" We can only guess at the sudden change in Haman's exuberance! As to Xerxes, it may seem strange that a short time before this, he had given Haman permission to write an edict ruling the annihilation of every Jew in his kingdom, but did you notice that Haman never named them? He never mentioned their ethnicity to the king. He referred to them only as a **certain race of people,** so Xerxes may not have ever made the connection.

So Haman took the robes and put them on Mordecai, placed him on the king's own horse, and led him through the city square, shouting,

"This is what the king does for someone he wishes to honor!"

Afterward Mordecai returned to the palace gate, but Haman hurried home dejected and completely humiliated.

We can only begin to imagine the desperate thoughts that must have been coursing through Haman's mind. A lot of emotion must have been churning between verses ten and eleven. When he learned that the one to be honored was anyone other than himself, that would be trial enough. Dressed as the king and paraded through the city on the king's horse while being lauded as one the king wants to honor would give the impression that he may be next in line for the throne. So anyone else being honored in this way would be a disappointment to Haman. But this was worse. Much worse. This was a Jew. This one that the king would honor was the very Jew who refused to bow to Haman. This was Mordecai! To say Haman was not happy is an understatement. Haman must have been enraged. And he couldn't show it.

Like it or not, Haman had to do what Haman had to do. It was the king's command.

Think about what was required to carry out the king's command. Haman had to go to the king's gate and tell Mordecai that his reward for loyalty to the king was being finally recognized. He was to be honored. Haman had to see to it that Mordecai was dressed in the king's royal robes. Then, Haman had to put Mordecai on the king's horse with the royal crest and parade him through the city, all the while shouting, *"This is what the king does for someone he wishes to honor!"* Everyone who knew that Mordecai was a Jew and had observed that he previously refused to bow to Haman would see it! How do you think that went for Haman?

What about Mordecai? How may he have felt about this whole *show?* Nothing had changed for him. He was still in mourning, still fasting, and still praying for the deliverance of his people. Now the author of his impending extermination was parading him through the city and praising him as one the king wanted to honor! It was likely evident to Mordecai that this was against Haman's will. Did Mordecai realize God was behind it? Could he have realized that this was the beginning of God's answer to his supplication? Mordecai was still facing death. A parade and praise were not on his mind. But God keeps His promises to those who honor Him.

"The LORD said to my Lord, "Sit in the place of honor at my right hand until I humble your enemies, making them a footstool under your feet."
Psalm 110:1

God often works in ways and by means we never expect. Our God is an awesome God!

As we wrap up this passage, we should consider the contrast between the circumstances of both Mordecai and Haman. We can note that Mordecai's ego was unaffected by all the pomp. We read that he returned to the king's gate to carry on his duty to the king. His service to the king. Haman's ego, however, was hugely affected by the events of the day. He was mortified! Head covered and embarrassed, and hoping no one would notice him, he made his way home. Remember, everyone was to bow to Haman, yet here we find him making every effort to avoid attention. Think of it. What Mordecai refused to do for Haman, Haman spent the whole day commanding others to do for Mordecai!

"My future is in your hands. Rescue me from those who hunt me down relentlessly." Psalm 31:15

A final thought. When Haman got home and told his wife and friends all that had transpired that day, their response was not what we might expect. They said, (more or less) "This guy is a Jew? You may as well prepare yourself for failure. You will never be successful in plotting harm against him! Let it go!"

Do you believe that even they recognized God's hand? Perhaps they had heard the stories of the Jews who were thrown in the fiery furnace to be burned alive and yet came out of it unharmed (Daniel 3). Or maybe they knew the story of Daniel being thrown into the lions den only to come out unharmed. (Daniel 6). If they didn't know the stories from Jewish neighbors, they likely knew much of the God of Israel from history. One thing is for sure: They seemed to know that the God of the Jews protects His people and that coming against them is a recipe for disaster.

Whether Haman considered their words, we do not know. It seems he really didn't have time to reconsider his evil intentions because, just as his friends finished speaking, the king's eunuchs appeared at his door to bring him to his second exclusive and private banquet with the king and queen. Off went Haman, likely stroking his ego as he was escorted to the palace.

My Treasure From God's Word...

_____

_____

_____

_____

_____

_____

_____

_____

_____

_____

"The kings of the earth prepare for battle; the rulers plot together against the LORD and against his anointed one...But the one who rules in heaven laughs. The Lord scoffs at them."
Psalm 2:2 and 4

Esther's Plea

Read: Esther 7:1-6

> *So the king and Haman went to Queen Esther's banquet. On this second occasion, while they were drinking wine, the king again said to Esther, "Tell me what you want, Queen Esther. What is your request? I will give it to you, even if it is half the kingdom!"*
>
> *Queen Esther replied, "If I have found favor with the king, and if it pleases the king to grant my request, I ask that my life and the lives of my people will be spared. For my people and I have been sold to those who would kill, slaughter, and annihilate us. If we had merely been sold as slaves, I could remain quiet, for that would be too trivial a matter to warrant disturbing the king."*
>
> *"Who would do such a thing?" King Xerxes demanded. "Who would be so presumptuous as to touch you?"*
>
> *Esther replied, "This wicked Haman is our adversary and our enemy." Haman grew pale with fright before the king and queen.*

Join me in imagining the scene. There Haman was among the opulence and luxury of the palace, sitting among soft billowy pillows on furniture covered in satin and fine linen, eating the most exotic of foods flavored by every kind of spice that may please the palate of the king, and sipping on the best of the best wines. Taking in all the pleasure of his surroundings, Haman could hear the intimate conversation passing between the king and his queen.

By the time of this second banquet, Xerxes must have been beyond curious. His attention fixed on Esther; he must have wondered what was so important that his queen would risk her life. He loved her and was prepared to give her whatever she desired.

As Haman continued to enjoy the meal, he heard Xerxes ask Queen Esther for a second time, **"What is your request? I will give it to you, even if it is half the kingdom!"** Esther had God-given wisdom to wait for the right time and place for the king to hear her request. God planned that an important event was to take place to prepare the king for this request. It was the discovery that Mordecai, the Jew, had never been rewarded for saving the king's life. Having prepared her heart over the course of many days, Esther was now ready for just **such a time as this.**

I wonder if, on that day, Esther felt brave. I am sure she felt a sense of both duty and urgency. It was very much a reality that she was risking her own life. Everything could flip against her if the king was not pleased with her request. At this point, neither he nor Haman knew that she was a Jew. She was about to uncover her secret. How would Xerxes receive such news?

Esther chose to trust God and do what was necessary for the good of her people, no matter the cost.

> **"Commit your actions to the LORD, and your plans will succeed."**
> Proverbs 16:3

> **"Faith is taking the first step even when you don't see the whole staircase."** —Martin Luther King Jr.

> **"There is no greater love than to lay down one's life for one's friends."**
> John 15:13

Esther didn't hesitate in presenting her request. I imagine her bowing before her husband as she carefully chose her words, **"If I have found favor with the king, and if it pleases the king to grant my request,"** then looking directly into her husband's eyes, she continued, **"I ask that my life and the lives of my people will be spared."** Then, tearfully and with intense sincerity, she finished, **"For my people and I have been sold to those who would kill, slaughter, and annihilate us. If we had merely been sold as slaves, I could remain quiet, for that would be too trivial a matter to warrant disturbing the king."** Esther, eyes to the ground again, waited for a response from the king.

Oh, to have such wisdom from God! It can be seen in when and where she presented her request and in how she carefully considered who should be present when she spoke these words to the king. It can be seen in how she used the exact words of Haman's edict and in how she considered what may be of importance to the king. And finally, it can be seen in how she delivered her request with an attitude of selflessness and humility. Esther's mission was to save the lives of her people and nothing less.

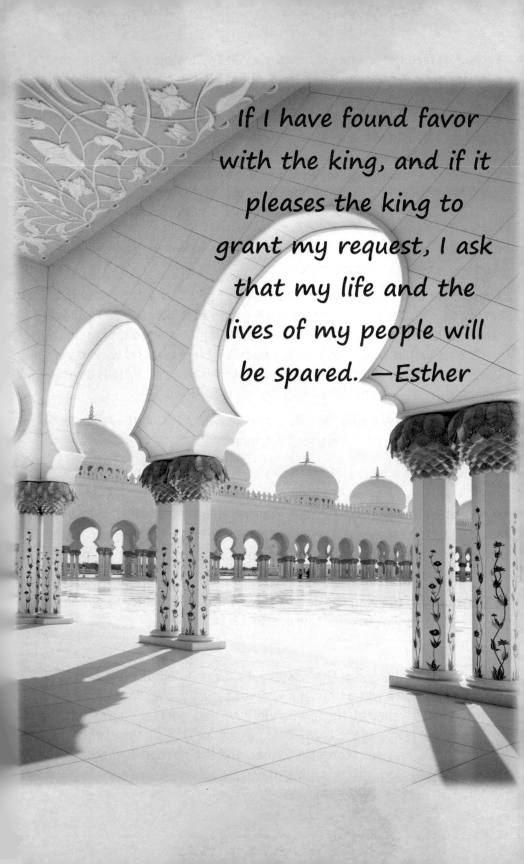

If I have found favor with the king, and if it pleases the king to grant my request, I ask that my life and the lives of my people will be spared. —Esther

Each of us face times when it seems people and factors we have no control over are deciding our course. At such times we can remind ourselves that for the child of God, nothing comes our way before it passes by our Father God. Comfort and courage of this truth can be found in many places in God's Word. Esther's story demonstrates this truth:

"So humble yourselves under the mighty power of God, and at the right time he will lift you up in honor. Give all your worries and cares to God, for he cares about you." 1 Peter 5:6-7

Queen Esther didn't know the end of the story as we do. She chose to trust God and step into His care anyway.

Esther's request utterly shocked Xerxes! He had effectively dealt with an attempt on his own life. How could his queen's life possibly be in danger? How had he not heard of this? Why hadn't Haman alerted him to this danger? Who would dare to touch the queen? Where was this wicked person who secretly plots murder? Who were Esther's *people*? Who is it that wants to annihilate an entire race? Xerxes was furious!

"With narrowed eyes, people plot evil; with a smirk, they plan their mischief." Proverbs 16:30

With these words, Esther's plight was suddenly very clear, and with these words, Haman's end was decided. *"It's Haman!"* Esther finally answered, as she pointed to the one the king most trusted. The wicked Haman, second to the king, had betrayed his trust and plotted the murder of the queen. All color draining from his face, Haman was suddenly terrified.

"The anger of the king is a deadly threat; the wise will try to appease it." Proverbs 16:14

As we come to the end of this passage, I am reminded of another king. It is King David. There was a time, many times actually, when he was being persecuted and pursued by those who were his own people. Like Esther, David called on the Name of the Lord. David asked for God's intervention. In their time of need, perhaps Mordecai, Esther, and their people had poured out their hearts to God with this same prayer:

"O Lord, oppose those who oppose me. Fight those who fight against me. Put on your armor, and take up your shield. Prepare for battle, and come to my aid. Lift up your spear and javelin against those who pursue me. Let me hear you say, "I will give you victory!" Bring shame and disgrace on those trying to kill me; turn them back and humiliate those who want to harm me. Blow them away like chaff in the wind—a wind sent by the angel of the Lord. Make their path dark and slippery, with the angel of the Lord pursuing them. I did them no wrong, but they laid a trap for me. I did them no wrong, but they dug a pit to catch me. So let sudden ruin come upon them! Let them be caught in the trap they set for me!"
Psalm 35:1-8

My Treasure From God's Word...

_____

_____

_____

_____

_____

_____

_____

_____

_____

_____

"You must worship only the Lord your God. He is the one
who will rescue you from all your enemies." 2 Kings 17:39

Haman's End

Read: Esther 7:7-10

Then the king jumped to his feet in a rage and went out into the palace garden.

Haman, however, stayed behind to plead for his life with Queen Esther, for he knew that the king intended to kill him. In despair he fell on the couch where Queen Esther was reclining, just as the king was returning from the palace garden.

The king exclaimed, "Will he even assault the queen right here in the palace, before my very eyes?" And as soon as the king spoke, his attendants covered Haman's face, signaling his doom.

Then Harbona, one of the king's eunuchs, said, "Haman has set up a sharpened pole that stands seventy-five feet tall in his own courtyard. He intended to use it to impale Mordecai, the man who saved the king from assassination."

"Then impale Haman on it!" the king ordered. So they impaled Haman on the pole he had set up for Mordecai, and the king's anger subsided.

Filled with rage, Xerxes stormed out into the garden. He needed time to think, time to process all that Esther has just said. His queen was a Jew—of the **certain race of people** his trusted advisor, Haman, planned to eliminate? How could this be? Was it completely true? He knew and trusted Esther, but could she be mistaken? His pride was likely hurt because he had trusted Haman. He would look like a fool for promoting Haman and giving him so much power. He had erred in approving the edict without weighing all the facts. In doing so, he had endangered two very special Jews, Mordecai, who saved his life, and Esther, his beloved wife.

"Spouting off before listening to the facts is both shameful and foolish."
Proverbs 18:13

"A wise man is cautious and turns away from evil, but a fool is arrogant and careless." Proverbs 14:16

Haman didn't follow the king into the garden. He remained where Esther was and began pleading with her for mercy—for his life. Knowing that the king would act swiftly, Haman, with no defense and overcome with fear, turned to Esther for help. Could he convince her? Begging for mercy, he fell across her couch just as Xerxes re-entered the hall. If Xerxes had considered extending any grace to this man, it ended with that sight! Was this man, Haman, assaulting and trying to silence the queen? This was too much!

Always nearby, the palace guards heard Esther's accusation, watched as the king stormed out to the garden, and watched as Haman groveled before the queen. Once in command of all the kingdom, Haman was now brought low by the uncovering of his wickedness.

Xerxes, had now caught him in a crime. It was well known that assaulting the queen would only end in death. Haman's doom was sure. **"Will he even assault the queen right here in the palace, before my very eyes?"** were Xerxes' words. As soon as the words were out of his mouth, the guards covered Haman's face. This was an indication to all of Haman's end.

It seems that Haman had been boasting about erecting the pole on which he would execute Mordecai. A servant knew of it and suggested to the king that this was how Haman should die. So it was that the very fate Haman planned for Mordecai became his end. At his home, in front of his family and friends, and visible to all of Susa.

"Don't be misled—you cannot mock the justice of God. You will always harvest what you plant." Galatians 6:7

"My experience shows that those who plant trouble and cultivate evil will harvest the same." Job 4:8

"The wicked conceive evil; they are pregnant with trouble and give birth to lies. They dig a deep pit to trap others, then fall into it themselves. The trouble they make for others backfires on them. The violence they plan falls on their own heads." Psalm 7:14-16

So they impaled Haman on the pole he had set up for Mordecai...

Chapter 7 ends with the words, **The king's anger subsided.** Haman was dead. Esther was safe. Xerxes thought he had saved the queen's life. On the surface, it seemed all was well, but we will see in the following pages that a problem remained. A big one. The Edict. According to the law of the Medes and the Persians, the edict was irreversible and irrevocable. The Jews were to be annihilated, and that could not be changed. Not even by the king.

My Treasure From God's Word...

_____

_____

_____

_____

_____

_____

_____

_____

_____

_____

"The godly are rescued from trouble, and it falls on the
wicked instead." Proverbs 11:8

"*Though I am surrounded by troubles, you will protect me from the anger of my enemies. You reach out your hand, and the power of your right hand saves me. The LORD will work out his plans for my life— for your faithful love, O LORD, endures forever. Don't abandon me, for you made me.*" Psalm 138:7-8

Part 3

The Edict

"God Has Made a Way!"

"The king's decree gave the Jews
in every city authority
to unite to defend their lives.
They were allowed to kill, slaughter, and annihilate anyone of any
nationality or province who might
attack them or their children and
wives, and to take the property of
their enemies."

Esther 8:11

Counteraction

Read: Esther 8:1-8

> *On that same day King Xerxes gave the property of Haman, the enemy of the Jews, to Queen Esther. Then Mordecai was brought before the king, for Esther had told the king how they were related. The king took off his signet ring—which he had taken back from Haman—and gave it to Mordecai. And Esther appointed Mordecai to be in charge of Haman's property.*
>
> *Then Esther went again before the king, falling down at his feet and begging him with tears to stop the evil plot devised by Haman the Agagite against the Jews. Again the king held out the gold scepter to Esther. So she rose and stood before him.*
>
> *Esther said, "If it please the king, and if I have found favor with him, and if he thinks it is right, and if I am pleasing to him, let there be a decree that reverses the orders of Haman son of Hammedatha the Agagite, who ordered that Jews throughout all the king's provinces should be destroyed. For how can I endure to see my people and my family slaughtered and destroyed?"*
>
> *Then King Xerxes said to Queen Esther and Mordecai the Jew, "I have given Esther the property of Haman, and he has been impaled on a pole because he tried to destroy the Jews. Now go ahead and send a message to the Jews in the king's name, telling them whatever you want, and seal it with the king's signet ring. But remember that whatever has already been written in the king's name and sealed with his signet ring can never be revoked.*

Our passage begins with these words: ***On that same day…*** As we read scripture, the amount of time passed is not always an important element for the clarity of the story, but that is not the case here. I am thinking of the amount of time that passed between Esther being taken from Mordecai's care, becoming queen, and the writing of the first edict. The number of years is not clear. But here, it seems God wants us to know that from the time Esther took that first step of faith by putting on her royal robes and going before the king, until now— was only three days! It seems significant,

Then Esther went again
before the king...

falling down at his feet and
begging him with tears...

as that is the exact number of days that she determined that she and all of Israel would fast and pray. Three days of calling on the Lord for wisdom, courage, and intervention and three days of doing all that she knew to do trusting that God in His mercy would bring it about. Esther had no idea how all of this would end, but she was willing to lay down her life for the cause.

> **"Anyone can believe when God is *already* moving, but real faith is when you step out when it seems that God is *not* moving."** — Reinhard Bonnke

So, ***that same day***. The day that Haman thought he would convince Xerxes to execute Mordecai. The day that Haman unknowingly advised the king of extravagant ways to honor Mordecai. The day Mordecai was greatly honored by Haman, followed by Haman creeping home in the shadows. The day that Esther gave her second banquet, revealing her ethnicity and pouring out her request to the king, The day that Xerxes learned the truth of the edict. The day that Haman met his end. ***That same day,*** the king gave Esther all that was Haman's. House, property, animals, and wealth. And on that God-ordained ***same day***, Xerxes embraced Mordecai as a member of the royal family, put him in charge of all of Esther's house, and gave him the signet ring. Position, power, and authority over all of Persia, given to Mordecai and Esther—Jews—***for such a time as this***.

Yet the edict remained. We read that ***Esther went again before the king, falling down at his feet and begging him with tears to stop the evil plot devised by Haman the Agagite against the Jews.*** I wonder if it was less frightening for her this time. The risk remained. Seeing Esther prostrate before him, tearfully pleading for the sake of her people, Xerxes held out the gold scepter to her once again. She needed to keep the fact of the edict before the king. She could not chance that this may be overlooked. Although she and Mordecai may have been under protection as members of the royal family, the danger to her people remained.

She stood before the king, and in absolute humility and submission, she began her request with, "If it pleases the king...if I have found favor with him...if the king thinks it's right...if I am pleasing to him, then, please, please reverse the decree, the edict, sent out by Haman that all my people and my family be destroyed!" Esther needed the king to know that she could not go on living as though this evil facing her people did not exist.

Then an amazingly wonderful, *only God could have planned it,* thing happened. The king gave Mordecai and Esther permission and authority to write another edict. They could write into law whatever was necessary to preserve the lives of their people—***for such a time as this!***

My Treasure From God's Word...

_____

_____

_____

_____

_____

_____

_____

_____

_____

_____

"A good man leaves an inheritance to his children's children, but the wealth of the sinner is stored up for the righteous."
Proverbs 13:22

The Plan

Read: Esther 8:9-17

So on June 25 the king's secretaries were summoned, and a decree was written exactly as Mordecai dictated. It was sent to the Jews and to the highest officers, the governors, and the nobles of all the 127 provinces stretching from India to Ethiopia. The decree was written in the scripts and languages of all the peoples of the empire, including that of the Jews. The decree was written in the name of King Xerxes and sealed with the king's signet ring. Mordecai sent the dispatches by swift messengers, who rode fast horses especially bred for the king's service.

The king's decree gave the Jews in every city authority to unite to defend their lives. They were allowed to kill, slaughter, and annihilate anyone of any nationality or province who might attack them or their children and wives, and to take the property of their enemies. The day chosen for this event throughout all the provinces of King Xerxes was March 7 of the next year.

A copy of this decree was to be issued as law in every province and proclaimed to all peoples, so that the Jews would be ready to take revenge on their enemies on the appointed day. So urged on by the king's command, the messengers rode out swiftly on fast horses bred for the king's service. The same decree was also proclaimed in the fortress of Susa.

Then Mordecai left the king's presence, wearing the royal robe of blue and white, the great crown of gold, and an outer cloak of fine linen and purple. And the people of Susa celebrated the new decree. The Jews were filled with joy and gladness and were honored everywhere. In every province and city, wherever the king's decree arrived, the Jews rejoiced and had a great celebration and declared a public festival and holiday. And many of the people of the land became Jews themselves, for they feared what the Jews might do to them.

The decree was written in the scripts and languages of all the peoples of the empire, including that of the Jews. The decree was written in the name of King Xerxes and sealed with the king's signet ring.

Now the Jews had a chance! Mordecai and Esther were to decide what the new edict would say! They knew they couldn't revoke or change Haman's evil plan, but what they could do was counteract it. They could write the new law to give the Jews a fighting chance.

Using the exact wording of Haman's law, they revised it to allow the Jews to defend themselves. They were not to be the aggressors, but if attacked, the new edict provided them with the right to assemble and defend them- selves. They also could take the possessions of those who attacked them. This was to be carried out on the same day as Haman's edict, March 7th of the following year. This gave the Jews 8 or 9 months to gather weapons, train for battle, and strategize. There was no question that some of the Persians would still attack, especially since they could also plunder, so the new version, although it allowed for the Jews' defense, would not deter the haters who were bent on their destruction.

This edict was written in every language and script of the empire and deliv- ered by messengers on swift horses. It was sent far and wide over the entire Persian empire, which at that time included areas from India to Ethiopia. It was a vast area. The highest officers, governors, and nobles in 127 provinces were made aware of the new law in favor of the Jews. Then, the work was done. It was in God's hands. How did the people respond? We are told of two groups.

The people of Mordecai and Esther—the Jews, realizing that God had heard their prayers and that deliverance was in their future—rejoiced! Once again, God had stepped into their story. Their faith was re-ignited. Their joy was restored. It was time for celebration. Feasting and holidays!

"You have turned my mourning into joyful dancing. You have taken away my clothes of mourning and clothed me with joy, that I might sing praises to you and not be silent. O LORD my God, I will give you thanks forever!"
Psalm 30:11-12

The people of Persia? Many of them were afraid. The tables had turned. The king had sided with the Jews. Haman was gone, and now this Jew, Mordecai, was in authority. What could they do? The gladness of the Jews had spread through the land. They seemed to think they had the upper hand. Maybe there was something to this God of the Jews. He had inter- cepted the plan to annihilate them in unimaginable ways. Maybe the smart thing to do would be to side with the Jews. Maybe then their God would protect a Persian too.

So, **many of the people of the land became Jews themselves**. They embraced the God of the Jews. And many hearts were changed. This was God's promise to Abraham many years prior. God has been at work all through history to bring about His promise that through the Jews all nations of the earth will be blessed.

"I will certainly bless you. I will multiply your descendants beyond number, like the stars in the sky and the sand on the seashore. Your descendants will conquer the cities of their enemies. And through your descendants all the nations of the earth will be blessed—all because you have obeyed me." Genesis 22:17-18

My Treasure From God's Word...

_____

_____

_____

_____

_____

_____

_____

_____

_____

_____

_____

_____

_____

_____

_____

_____

_____

_____

_____

_____

"Those who have been ransomed by the LORD will return. They will enter Jerusalem singing, crowned with everlasting joy. Sorrow and mourning will disappear, and they will be filled with joy and gladness." Isaiah 51:11

Self-defense

Read: Esther 9:1-18

So on March 7 the two decrees of the king were put into effect. On that day, the enemies of the Jews had hoped to overpower them, but quite the opposite happened. It was the Jews who overpowered their enemies. The Jews gathered in their cities throughout all the king's provinces to attack anyone who tried to harm them. But no one could make a stand against them, for everyone was afraid of them. And all the nobles of the provinces, the highest officers, the governors, and the royal officials helped the Jews for fear of Mordecai. For Mordecai had been promoted in the king's palace, and his fame spread throughout all the provinces as he became more and more powerful.

So the Jews went ahead on the appointed day and struck down their enemies with the sword. They killed and annihilated their enemies and did as they pleased with those who hated them. In the fortress of Susa itself, the Jews killed 500 men. They also killed Parshandatha, Dalphon, Aspatha, Poratha, Adalia, Aridtha, Parmashta, Arisai, Aridai, and Vaizatha— the ten sons of Haman son of Hammedatha, the enemy of the Jews. But they did not take any plunder.

That very day, when the king was informed of the number of people killed in the fortress of Susa, he called for Queen Esther. He said, "The Jews have killed 500 men in the fortress of Susa alone, as well as Haman's ten sons. If they have done that here, what has happened in the rest of the provinces? But now, what more do you want? It will be granted to you; tell me and I will do it."

Esther responded, "If it please the king, give the Jews in Susa permission to do again tomorrow as they have done today, and let the bodies of Haman's ten sons be impaled on a pole."

So the king agreed, and the decree was announced in Susa. And they impaled the bodies of Haman's ten sons. Then the Jews at Susa gathered together on March 8 and killed 300 more men, and again they took no plunder.

Meanwhile, the other Jews throughout the king's provinces had gathered together to defend their lives. They gained relief from all their enemies, killing 75,000 of those who hated them. But they did not take any plunder. This was done throughout the provinces on March 7, and on March 8 they rested, celebrating their victory with a day of feasting and gladness. (The Jews at Susa killed their enemies on March 7 and again on March 8, then rested on March 9, making that their day of feasting and gladness.)

This is perhaps the most difficult part of Esther's story. Difficult to understand, embrace, and imagine. Yet, it had been by the command of our holy God that the Amalekite nation, the people of King Agag, be completely and thoroughly destroyed (Exodus 17:14-16). Although many who died in attacking the Jews in Persia were not of Amalekite descent, they had been influenced by their hatred of the Jews, greedy for their possessions, and like the Amalekites, demonstrated no fear of God.

The Jew haters of Persia had eleven months to plan for the 7th of March. Since they were given permission, even enticed to take the Jews possessions, they had time to consider which Jews would be the *easiest pickings* and who were most hated. There was a lot of time for the hatred to ripen. Consider this: the Jews could kill only those who attacked them. 75 thousand people attacked the Jews. How do we know? Because the Jews legally killed 75 thousand people throughout the provinces. God had intervened through Mordecai's edict. The people of Persia did not have to kill the Jews. They could have chosen another way. Through Mordecai, God had made a way for them too.

"When all the surrounding kingdoms heard that the Lord himself had fought against the enemies of Israel, the fear of God came over them."
2 Chronicles 20:29.

This was God's *way out* for those haters of Israel. God caused them to be afraid of both the Jews and the powerful position of Mordecai. Yet there were plenty in the land who hardened their hearts and chose to attack the Jews anyway. By this, they became the enemies of God.

On that day, the enemies of the Jews had hoped to over-power them, but quite the opposite happened. It was the Jews who overpowered their enemies.

The scripture tells us that many in leadership positions actually assisted the Jews. They knew that Mordecai was the king's choice and that the king had given him authority. To side with the Jews was to show loyalty to the king. So they gave respect and honor to Mordecai as a member of the royal family and as the one the king chose to honor. In reality, it was God who gave Mordecai this high position, respect, and authority. Mordecai, with great wisdom and humility, used his authority to faithfully do the will of God. God used Mordecai to save His people from destruction.

On the 7th of March, the day chosen for their annihilation, the Jews throughout all of Persia killed everyone who attacked them. Their motivation was defense. Protection of life. When we think of such killing, it seems murderous and is horrific, but on this day **the Jew's motivation was not murder but self-defense.** In the fortress itself, the Jews killed five hundred who came against them, including the ten sons of Haman.

When Xerxes received the report of five hundred being killed in Susa this time, it was he who called for Esther. If there were five hundred Jew haters in Susa, how many more must there have been throughout the entire kingdom? How many more were not loyal to their king? Was there anything more his queen wished to be done?

Esther's request was for another day. Haman had many friends in Susa. There were likely many more. So, Esther requested that the Jews would be permitted to kill anyone who attacked them on a second day and that Haman's ten sons, although already dead be impaled and publicly displayed for all to see and fear. The king extended Mordecai's edict one more day, and three hundred more people in Susa came against the Jews—right there in the king's city, even though Haman's edict had expired. And so, they too met their end.

As we come to the last verses of the passage, I want to point out something that may be overlooked. We have read three different times that the Jews **took no plunder,** even though the edict had given them the freedom to do so. Perhaps they remembered the mistake King Saul had made when God told him to destroy everything that had anything to do with the Amalekites. Instead, King Saul allowed King Agag to live and kept the best of his livestock for Israel. The Jews would have known this from history, and on this day, perhaps they chose to finally honor God's command. By this truth, we can know that **the Jews were not motivated by greed but rather, by gratitude.** The Lord had made a way for them. With hearts of thankfulness for their salvation, they did not need the stuff of the enemy.

God had made a way.

As the passage ends, we understand that the killing ended throughout the empire on March 7th and the people rested. Everywhere but Susa. Queen Esther, with God-given wisdom, saw to it that the Jew haters in Susa were defeated on a second day. And then there was peace. Celebrations of feasting and gladness followed for all who feared the God of the Jews.

"We were filled with laughter, and we sang for joy. And the other nations said, 'What amazing things the LORD has done for them.'" Psalm 126:2

My Treasure From God's Word...

_____

_____

_____

_____

_____

_____

_____

_____

_____

_____

_____

_____

_____

_____

_____

_____

_____

_____

"...I will give you a new heart, and I will put a new spirit in you. I will take out your stony, stubborn heart and give you a tender, responsive heart. And I will put my Spirit in you so that you will follow my decrees and be careful to obey my regulations." Ezekial 36:26-27

Purim

Read: Esther 9:19-30

So to this day, rural Jews living in remote villages celebrate an annu-al festival and holiday on the appointed day in late winter, when they rejoice and send gifts of food to each other.

Mordecai recorded these events and sent letters to the Jews near and far, throughout all the provinces of King Xerxes, calling on them to celebrate an annual festival on these two days. He told them to celebrate these days with feasting and gladness and by giving gifts of food to each other and presents to the poor. This would commem-orate a time when the Jews gained relief from their enemies, when their sorrow was turned into gladness and their mourning into joy.

So the Jews accepted Mordecai's proposal and adopted this annual custom. Haman son of Hammedatha the Agagite, the enemy of the Jews, had plotted to crush and destroy them on the date determined by casting lots (the lots were called purim). But when Esther came before the king, he issued a decree causing Haman's evil plot to backfire, and Haman and his sons were impaled on a sharpened pole. That is why this celebration is called Purim, because it is the ancient word for casting lots.

So because of Mordecai's letter and because of what they had expe-rienced, the Jews throughout the realm agreed to inaugurate this tradition and to pass it on to their descendants and to all who be-came Jews. They declared they would never fail to celebrate these two prescribed days at the appointed time each year. These days would be remembered and kept from generation to generation and celebrated by every family throughout the provinces and cities of the empire. This Festival of Purim would never cease to be celebrated among the Jews, nor would the memory of what happened ever die out among their descendants.

Then Queen Esther, the daughter of Abihail, along with Mordecai the Jew, wrote another letter putting the queen's full authority be-hind Mordecai's letter to establish the Festival of Purim. Letters

wishing peace and security were sent to the Jews throughout the
127 provinces of the empire of Xerxes.

As we read to the end of chapter nine, we get a better understanding of the reason for the Jewish holiday called **Purim**. We get a bit more details too. Even to this day as I write, in the year 2024, the Jewish people honor and celebrate the 14th and 15th of Adar (by the Hebrew calendar) as a time for feasting and celebration. It is called **Purim,** as in the Babylonian language, this means *the casting of lots*. The term we may use today is *rolling of the dice*.

As was stated earlier, Haman decided the day of the Jew's annihilation by the casting of lots. The casting of lots was a form of astrology, and important decisions required consulting the stars. We also know that although this was Haman's method of choosing the future, the God of Isael, Creator of heaven, earth, and all things, in His sovereignty can intercept and overrule all and any plan for evil. And He did just that in Esther's story.

He did it in my story too. He will do it in yours.

So, Purim from that day to this is a time for feasting and gladness. Why? To remember the deliverance of God! To remember a time when the Jews, experiencing the depths of great sorrow and facing sure destruction, were given a chance to live! Their sorrow was turned to gladness. How? By God's intervention using two ordinary people, Mordecai and Esther, who were willing to step out into the unknown, knowing that their God is mighty to save!

"The Spirit of the Sovereign LORD is upon me, for the LORD has anointed me to bring good news to the poor. He has sent me to comfort the broken-hearted and to proclaim that captives will be released and prisoners will be freed. He has sent me to tell those who mourn that the time of the LORD's favor has come, and with it, the day of God's anger against their enemies. To all who mourn in Israel, he will give a crown of beauty for ashes, a joyous blessing instead of mourning, festive praise instead of despair. In their righteousness, they will be like great oaks that the LORD has planted for his own glory." Isaiah 61:1-3

Although written to and about the Jewish nation of Israel, these beautiful words are also for anyone who has been adopted into God's family. And

Purim

This would commemorate a time when the Jews gained relief from their enemies, when their sorrow was turned into gladness and their mourning into joy.

that includes you if you have put your faith and hope in Jesus, the Messiah of Israel!

Mordecai recorded all of this in a book (which may be why we have a record of "Esther") and sent out letters to Jews throughout the empire declaring these two days be holidays for the Jews everywhere throughout every generation. They were to celebrate with feasting and gladness. They prepared special foods and enjoyed gift-giving. At a later time, this was further endorsed and solidified by Queen Esther as she sent letters of peace and security to all Jews throughout the kingdom.

Current-day Jews gather in synagogues for the reading of the book of Esther on the 13th of Adar every year. At every mention of the name Haman, they cry out, "May he be accursed!" They also fast on that day. On the 14th of Adar, they once again gather in the synagogue. This day is a reading of the story of Moses and the Amalekites (Exodus 17:8-16), followed by the book of Esther being read a second time. A joyous meal of special foods is shared by all, and then there is gift-giving. The celebration continues a third day with more gift-giving, especially to the poor. This is how the Jewish people commemorate this time of God's deliverance and rescue of the Jewish nation and pass it down to every generation.

You see, the one who meant this for evil has been working throughout history to thwart God's plan. The goal of Satan is to stop God's plan of salvation. It is his aim to stop the Messiah, God's rescue plan for man. Influenced by Satan, Haman's scheme against the Jews could have destroyed the Jewish nation. God's plan was to send salvation through Jesus—a Jew. We see Satan at work again when Jesus was born, as Herod ordered all Jewish males under two years to be killed (Matthew 2:16), and finally with Judas' betrayal of Jesus (Luke 22:3-4), which resulted in the crucifixion of Jesus. It seemed that evil had prevailed. Satan began his interference in the Garden of Eden, and he won't stop until the end. But, as it was with Haman, Satan will meet his end.

"Nothing is a surprise to God. Nothing is a problem for God. Nothing is a mistake by God. Anything is possible with God."
—Ann Voskamp

From God's perspective, the battle with evil is already won. Those who put their hope and trust in Jesus' death, burial, and resurrection are the victors. Friend, by trusting in Jesus, we have already won!

"Then I heard again what sounded like the shout of a vast crowd
or the roar of mighty ocean waves or the crash of loud thunder:
"Praise the LORD!
For the Lord our God, the Almighty, reigns.
Let us be glad and rejoice, and let us give honor to him.
For the time has come for the wedding feast of the Lamb..."

Revelation 19:6-7

My Treasure From God's Word...

_____

_____

_____

_____

_____

_____

_____

_____

_____

_____

_____

_____

_____

_____

_____

_____

_____

"I heard a loud shout from the throne, saying, "Look, God's home is now among his people! He will live with them, and they will be his people. God himself will be with them. He will wipe every tear from their eyes, and there will be no more death or sorrow or crying or pain. All these things are gone forever." Revelation 21:3-4

Legacy

Read: Esther 10

> *King Xerxes imposed a tribute throughout his empire, even to the*
> *distant coastlands. His great achievements and the full account of*
> *the greatness of Mordecai, whom the king had promoted, are rec-*
> *orded in The Book of the History of the Kings of Media and*
> *Persia. Mordecai the Jew became the prime minister, with authori-*
> *ty next to that of King Xerxes himself. He was very great among*
> *the Jews, who held him in high esteem, because he continued to*
> *work for the good of his people and to speak up for the welfare of*
> *all their descendants.*

The Book of Esther comes to an end with chapter 10. Despite containing only three verses, it provides some important details. A new tribute or tax was imposed by King Xerxes. It would take effect throughout the entire empire. This included distant islands that belonged to Persia. Likely there was a need to replace finances lost during the failed attempt to conquer Greece. There has been some speculation that perhaps this new tax was Mordecai's idea. Until this time, most revenue was obtained through wars and plundering. In order to further protect his people, perhaps Mordecai suggested a tax be imposed on all people throughout the empire. This would alleviate the need for violent *collection,* and since the Jews under Mordecai's rule were flourishing and prosperous, this idea may have made sense to Xerxes.

Next, we read of the recordings in the Book of the History of the Kings of Media and Persia. Of course, prideful Xerxes saw to it that his exploits and accomplishments were recorded for all future generations to read, but to our great astonishment, we also read that the greatness of Mordecai the Jew was recorded too! From *history,* we can know that *The Book of Esther* is not just a *story.* God ordained it to be recorded for our benefit. From this, we can know that:

Mordecai was a real man who, lived in Persia, served the king, was pro-
moted by the king, and sought the good of the Jewish people.

Mordecai was a man who through faith in God, interceded for the Jewish people and brought peace and prosperity to the Jewish people of Persia.

We would be overlooking the most important character in this story if we were not to mention another. Never once is His name mentioned, but His presence and activity are obvious throughout *The Book of Esther*. That One is God. Apart from His intervention, the Jews would have had no future and no hope.

Sometimes God puts people in positions they would never dream of applying for. That was true for both Mordecai and Esther. When it came time to intercede on behalf of their people, they recognized that it was in their hands to make a difference. It was through faith and reliance on God that they did just that. They couldn't change Haman's wicked law, but with God's help and great wisdom, they inscribed a new law that protected the Jewish people. By laying aside personal risk and making courageous choices, Mordecai and Esther were used by God to continue His plan, which would eventually give us the Savior. I wonder if C.S. Lewis was thinking of them when he penned these words:

"You can't go back and change the beginning but you can start where you are and change the ending." —C.S. Lewis

With God's help and by His favor, that is what Mordecai and Esther did. And from that time until now, the choices they made for the peace and prosperity of their people are remembered, learned from, and celebrated.

- Just as Mordecai adopted and protected Esther, Jesus adopts and protects all who come to Him for forgiveness of sin.

- Just as Mordecai mourned over the destruction that was coming to his people, Jesus mourned over the destruction people reap as the result of sin.

- Just as Mordecai was appointed and empowered by the king to save his people, Jesus was appointed and empowered by God to save the world.

- Just as Mordecai created a new law that saved his people, God created a new law to save all people—Jesus is the way. Put your trust in Him.

Mordecai the Jew became the prime minister, with authority next to that of King Xerxes himself. He was very great among the Jews, who held him in high esteem, because he continued to work for the good of his people and to speak up for the welfare of all their descendants.

Mordecai's story is a foreshadowing of Jesus. All who embrace the new law of salvation by grace through faith in Jesus—will live.

"Yes, I am the gate. Those who come in through me will be saved. They will come and go freely and will find good pastures. The thief's purpose is to steal and kill and destroy. My purpose is to give them a rich and satisfying life. " John 10:9-10

◆ Just as Mordecai became great and was respected among the people, every knee will bow in heaven and earth and under the earth at the Name of Jesus.

◆ Just as Mordecai sought the good of his people, Jesus laid down His life for all people.

◆ Just as Mordecai's greatness was recorded by the king in his book, Jesus' greatness is recorded by the King in the greatest book of all, the Bible.

You see, the Old Testament and the New Testament are one and the same. Just as God loved His people, Israel, and wanted relationship with them and obedience from them, so Jesus wants the same with us. The message throughout both testaments is this:

God is. God loves you. God wants a relationship with you. God expects you to live a life of obedience to Him.

God made a covenant or promise to Israel. He said He would multiply and bless them. He promised that all the families of the earth would be blessed *through* them. With that, He gave them an outward sign or symbol that they belonged to Him. It was circumcision. That was a fleshly sign, but the spiritual meaning was that they were set apart to Him and for Him. It was a change of the heart.

"The **Lord** *your God will change your heart and the hearts of all your descendants, so that you will love him with all your heart and soul and so you may live!"* Deuteronomy 30:6.

And in time, He promised to write it on their hearts.

"But this is the covenant that I will make with the house of Israel after those days, says the **Lord***: I will put My law in their minds, and write it on their hearts; and I will be their God, and they shall be My people."* Jeremiah 31:33.

And yet, we know that all through the Old Testament, the people of Israel broke God's law. Time and time again, they failed woefully. Although God offered relationship, fellowship, and enjoyment of a life lived in obedience to Him, they could not maintain it.

And neither can we. This poses a problem. You see, disobedience to God's law is sin. Since God is holy and without sin, this separates us from God.

"If I regard sin and baseness in my heart [that is, if I know it is there and do nothing about it], The Lord will not hear [me];" Psalm 66:18 AMP.

We lose access to God. So, in mercy and kindness, God made a different way— a new way—a new covenant. And that my friend is found in His Son, the Lord Jesus. We have access to God through faith in Him.

"I am the way, the truth, and the life. No one can come to the Father except through me." John 14:6

My Treasure From God's Word...

_____

_____

_____

_____

_____

_____

_____

_____

_____

_____

_____

_____

_____

_____

_____

_____

_____

_____

_____

_____

"Furthermore, we have seen with our own eyes and now testify that the Father sent his Son to be the Savior of the world." 1 John 4:14

Part 4

The Edict

"Jesus is the Way!"

"So now there is no condemnation for those who belong to Christ Jesus.

And because you belong to him, the power of the life-giving Spirit has freed you from the power of sin that leads to death."

Romans 8:1-2

It is Finished!

The main thing is to keep the main thing the main thing."— Stephen Covey

I have attempted to do that in this study. As in all of the Bible, throughout this story, there is one *main thing*, one main idea, one theme, which is God's rescue plan for men. It leads us to the Messiah, the Savior of the world, the Lord Jesus Christ.

Here in these final pages we will consider truths that were alluded to throughout. You see, **The Book of Esther** is part of God's bigger story—the plan of salvation. In the end, it is part of the story of every person that God created.

From the first sin, as Adam and Eve ate from the one tree that God had forbidden—the sinful downward spiral of all men was set into motion. God has always wanted a relationship with His creation. He created us for such, but mankind chooses to disobey. In the beginning, the Creator gave only one, **"Thou shalt not."** In all the garden, there was only one law. Yet His created ones chose to go their own way. Our merciful God set into motion a plan to redeem His creation—a rescue—a Savior—the Lord Jesus.

From the first days of creation until this very day, Satan, the enemy of our souls, has worked to interfere with and prevent our relationship with our Creator. He has been successful too. Through Adam's sin, sin entered the world. With sin came death. The result of sin is that all of us—each one—is facing death—eternal separation from God.

"When Adam sinned, sin entered the world. Adam's sin brought death, so death spread to everyone, for everyone sinned." Romans 5:12

You see, as in Mordecai's day, God's laws cannot be reversed or revoked. His laws are always right and just. God is holy, blameless, and cannot look at sin. God's law is that sin must be punished. The punishment for sin is death. It is eternal separation from God. That poses a problem.

"For everyone has sinned; we all fall short of God's glorious standard."
Romans 3:23

"As the Scriptures say, 'No one is righteous—not even one. No one is truly wise; no one is seeking God. All have turned away; all have become useless. No one does good, not a single one.'" Romans 3:10-12

All have sinned. Everyone. Compared to God's holiness, there is no one who is good. No, not one. So, death came into God's perfect world with that first sin and was passed down from generation to generation. This is a problem for all people. Since we break God's **edict**, His **law** (because all have sinned), God, in His mercy, counteracted His law. **He made another way. A new law.** We are offered access to God through His Son, Jesus. Jesus is our way. Through Him we find forgiveness of sin. Jesus is our rescue, our way of salvation.

"When we were utterly helpless, Christ came at just the right time and died for us sinners. Now, most people would not be willing to die for an upright person, though someone might perhaps be willing to die for a person who is especially good. But God showed his great love for us by sending Christ to die for us while we were still sinners. And since we have been made right in God's sight by the blood of Christ, he will certainly save us from God's condemnation." Romans 5:6-9

Jesus is God's gift of grace to men. Grace is unmerited favor. It is something we did not earn. Just as God gave Esther *favor* with the king, so God has given us favor by sending His Son.

God saved you by his grace when you believed. And you can't take credit for this; it is a gift from God. Salvation is not a reward for the good things we have done, so none of us can boast about it. Ephesians 2:8-9

You see, the rescue or salvation is not only in Jesus' coming *to live in our world*, but more importantly, He came *to die for our world*. God's law requires punishment for sin. So, in great love and mercy, He sent His sinless Son to take our punishment. He came to die in our place. He came to die for me. He came to die for you. Specifically for the sins we have committed. Jesus took our punishment on Himself on the cross.

"Christ suffered for our sins once for all time. He never sinned, but he died for sinners to bring you safely home to God." 1 Peter 3:18

God's law required a blood sacrifice for sin. Jesus was that sacrifice when He died on the cross. He took on Himself the sins of the world, and He did this so that we could be forgiven and have a restored relationship with God.

"It is finished " were His words. With those words, the transaction was complete. Our sin in exchange for His righteousness! What appeared to be the end, was only the beginning. Jesus did die for us but now He lives for us!

"For God made Christ, who never sinned, to be the offering for our sin, so that we could be made right with God through Christ." 2 Corinthians 5:21

Now. I have a question for you. What will you do with what you have learned in this study?

God is our King. His law is unchangeable and irrevocable. It declares that the wage or payment for sin is death. No one can escape this truth.

"...it is appointed for men to die once and after this comes judgment, " Hebrews 9:27 NASB.

However, God, in His great love, extended His grace (favor) to us by creating a new law. God has made a way of rescue for you and me. And that is through faith in His Son, Jesus.

"For this is how God loved the world: He gave his one and only Son, so that everyone who believes in him will not perish but have eternal life." John 3:16

"God chose him as your ransom long before the world began..." 1 Peter 1:20

If you have not already done so, won't you accept God's gift of salvation through Jesus today?

Agree with God that you are a sinner.

Believe. Believe that Jesus died, was buried, and rose again. Believe that He died for your sins. Believe that God loves you and will forgive you. *"If you confess with your mouth that Jesus is Lord and believe in your heart that God raised him from the dead, you will be saved. For it is by believing in your heart that you are made right with God, and it is by confessing with your mouth that you are saved."* Romans 10:9-10

Confess your sin. *"If we confess our sins, He is faithful and just to forgive us our sins and to cleanse us from all unrighteousness."* 1 John 1:9

My Treasure From God's Word...

_____

_____

_____

_____

_____

_____

_____

_____

_____

_____

_____

_____

_____

_____

_____

_____

_____

_____

"You were cleansed from your sins when you obeyed the truth, so now you must show sincere love to each other as brothers and sisters. Love each other deeply with all your heart. For you have been born again, but not to a life that will quickly end. Your new life will last forever because it comes from the eternal, living word of God...But the Word of the Lord remains forever. And that word is the Good News that was preached to you." 1 Peter 1:22-23, 25

About the author...

Robin Ivins is a wife, mother, and grandmother, and follower of Christ. She enjoys time spent with family, travel, photography, and writing.

Robin and her husband, Bob, were involved in church building in Siberia, Russia for several years, and most recently, served men in rehabilitation and discipleship at <u>Transformation Life Center</u>, West Park, NY.

This is Robin's second published book. The first, *Rebuilding...Begins on Our Knees* was published in 2023. It is a study of the book of Nehemiah.

For more information, you may reach them through their Facebook ministry page:

<u>The Ripple Effect: Bob & Robin Ivins</u>

This book was published by Purebooks Publishing Company which is a part of Kelly's Complete Digital Design.

KELLYAULNOVELS.COM

Made in the USA
Columbia, SC
13 November 2024

46169057R00087